Berg ten, Staffan, 1932–
Öst Sjöstrand. New York, Twayne
Publish [1974]
    174 p. t. 21 cm. (Twayne's world
authors ser TWAS 309. Sweden)
Bibliography: p. 167 70.
ISBN 0-8057-2844-9

1. Sjöstrand, Östen. I. Title.

TWAYNE'S WORLD AUTHORS SERIES

A Survey of the World's Literature

Sylvia E. Bowman, Indiana University

GENERAL EDITOR

SWEDEN

Leif Sjöberg, State University of New York, Stony Brook

EDITOR

Östen Sjöstrand

(TWAS 309)

Photo by Lufti Özkök

Osten Sjöstrand

Östen Sjöstrand

By STAFFAN BERGSTEN

University of Uppsala

Twayne Publishers, Inc.   ::   New York

Library of Congress Cataloging in Publication Data

Bergsten, Staffan, 1932–
  Östen Sjöstrand.

  (Twayne's world authors series, TWAS 309. Sweden)
  Bibliography: p. 167.
  1. Sjöstrand, Östen.
PT9875.S58Z6   839.7'1'74   74-574
ISBN 0-8057-2844-9

Contents

About the Author

Staffan Bergsten, who was born in 1932, holds a doctorate from the University of Uppsala and his inaugural dissertation was published in 1960 under the title *Time and Eternity: A Study in the Structure and Symbolism of T.S. Eliot's Four Quartets* (reissued in New York, 1974). In 1957–58 he was lecturer of Swedish at Cambridge University. Since 1960 he has lectured in, and is currently head of the department of literary history at the University of Uppsala.

Among his published works are a study on the Swedish Romantic poet Erik Johan Stagnelius (*Erotikern Stagnelius*, Stockholm, 1966), a book on Cosmic Analogies in Twentieth Century Swedish Poetry (*Jaget och världen*, Uppsala, 1971) and contributions to various periodicals and textbooks. Since 1965 he regularly contributes talks on literary topics to the Swedish Broadcasting Company.

＊　＊　＊　＊

The translations of Sjöstrand's poems were made by Robin Fulton in close collaboration with the poet himself. A selection from Sjöstrand's poetic work with parallel Swedish and English text, *The Hidden Music*, has recently been published by Oleander Press, New York.

Dr. Fulton, of Edinburgh, is himself a poet, critic, and editor of the *Lines Review*. Currently he fulfills the duties of lecturer in English at the University of Stavanger, Norway.

Preface

Although the poetry of Östen Sjöstrand may as yet be little known outside his native Sweden, this book has been written in the belief that with a wider knowledge of his work a recognition of the originality and importance of his contribution to both Swedish and international literature will surely follow. If his work were already more familiar than it is, then the obvious approach would be to offer a general critical evaluation. Since, however, one of the principal aims has been to introduce Sjöstrand to a wider public, the approach has been to concentrate more objectively on the questions how and why rather than on the question how good. Nevertheless, it should be clear that in the course of the study sufficient critical emphasis is made to indicate the possible lines of an evaluation.

As a historical phenomenon, each work of art may be explained in terms of two sets of causes, one relating to the artist's private world, his personal background and inner experience, his dreams and visions; the other relating to the social and cultural tradition to which the work of art belongs once it is created. This applies to most creative work, no doubt, but what is worth special consideration in Sjöstrand's case is the balance between the two sets of causes. A work of art that can be exhausted by referring it to a particular genre, tradition, or cultural environment is, in its lack of originality, of limited interest. On the other hand, a work so original as to be wholly unrelated to any established tradition or cultural context is of equally small interest. The too typical is boring because it is too well understood, the unique irritates because it is incomprehensible. Internationally, Sjöstrand has the advantage of relying on a common European literary heritage, which should make him readily accessible even to those totally unfamiliar with his national background. And if his nationally and personally conditioned qualities are found somewhat more difficult to understand, that too is perhaps an advantage.

The poetic tradition to which Sjöstrand belongs is the one that was foreshadowed by the early nineteenth-century Romantics, made conscious and deliberate by the Symbolists, developed, distorted, twisted, perverted, rejuvenated, and still further developed by Modernists of every kind and description; a very heterogeneous, even a confused tradition, yet still a tradition which went through a somewhat belated but very vital phase in Swedish letters during the 1940's, when Sjöstrand entered the literary scene. Producing his first book of poetry in 1949, he was a latecomer to that belated phase of Modernism which had culminated some years earlier in Sweden and a decade or two earlier in Europe generally. This would seem the typical starting-point for an epigone, but Sjöstrand turned the situation to his advantage and set out to develop new branches on the old tree of Modernism while many of his fellow writers took to the ground in search of conventional idyls, or social realism, or political commitment. In consequence he became an isolated figure for many years, not quite neglected but little understood. Yet out of this partially neglected early work has grown a rich and mature body of poetry which is attracting increasing attention. Born in 1925, Sjöstrand is still only in middle life and we have every reason to expect further developments of his art.

Much of his poetic work can be explained in terms of the Modernist tradition, but not its distinguishing features, which are the reflections of his particular personality and background. Without his early encounters with music, science, and religion he would never have pressed the frontiers of poetry as he has done in the direction of the most recent ideas in these fields. Without being exposed, as a youth, to bereavement and emotional distress, he would never have entered manhood with that lack of inner stability which alone permits the creative artist, often at the cost of great suffering, to keep his mind and senses open to experiences from which other people guard themselves as alien and dangerous to a "normal" life.

That is what Sjöstrand's work looks like regarded with the cool and critical eye of the literary historian: the effect of the confrontation of a particular temperament and personality with a given poetic tradition. But Sjöstrand himself would hardly be satisfied with a critical approach which limited itself to historical and causal relations. He would assert the rights of any such work to be interpreted and judged as an independent esthetic structure, and he would also express his conviction, or hope, that poetry—his own poetry, any poetry worth the name—partakes of a timeless, archetypal dimension of existence where all men can join in a common understanding of the conditions of human life. In the present study, such claims will be analyzed and interpreted within their historical and psychological framework.

So far nothing has been said to justify the selection of Sjöstrand out of the multitude of contemporary Swedish poets— lyrical poetry has always been the forte of Swedish literature, while in fiction and drama it is rather more derivative—nothing except a claim to originality and importance still to be specified. Sjöstrand's original contribution—if such it is—can be specified under three separate headings. First, his achievements in the way of formal development of poetic language, particularly his use of music as a source of inspiration and structural models. Secondly, his integrating of modern science into the imagery and subject matter of his poetry. And thirdly and perhaps most important, his concern with the future of man on earth, with our natural environment and cultural heritage, both equally threatened. After the general, chronological outline of Sjöstrand's life and work in Chapter 1, each of these three aspects of his work will be treated separately in Chapters 2–4.

A word should be added concerning the texts and translations reproduced in the course of the following study. Some of Sjöstrand's poems have appeared in different English translations, but only those by Robin Fulton have been used here, not only because his translations form the most comprehensive selection of Sjöstrand's work but because he has worked them out in close contact with the poet himself.

Dr. Fulton has done much to facilitate my work, supplying bits of poetic translations when needed and reading the whole of my manuscript with a view to stylistic improvements so valuable to one writing in an acquired language. I give my thanks to him and to three others who have contributed facts, stimulation, and encouragement: Sven-Erik Bäck, the composer; Maria Pettersson, the poet's sister; and Östen Sjöstrand himself, who has that ability rare among poets and artists, to submit himself and his work to the sometimes skeptical analysis of scholarly inquiry without trying to force his own interpretations and evaluations upon the writer, without doubting, even in the face of adverse criticism, the friendship that made this book possible.

STAFFAN BERGSTEN

University of Uppsala

Acknowledgments

For permission to quote extensively from Östen Sjöstrand's poetry and essays I am indebted to his publisher, Albert Bonniers förlags AB, Stockholm, and to Professor Ronald Bates and the editor of *Mosaic* for their permission to use materials first published in that journal.

I also wish to express my gratitude to the Swedish Institute and to Längmanska Stiftelsen, Stockholm, for their generous grants, which made the English translation of Sjöstrand's poetry possible.

Chronology

1884   Oscar Pettersson, Sjöstrand's father, born.

1899   Ebba Larsson Gumeer, his mother, born.

1909   Oscar (Pettersson) Sjöstrand becomes a school teacher in Gothenburg.

1920   (ca.) Oscar Sjöstrand goes into business with the publishing firm Nordiska Förlags AB.

1924   Oscar Sjöstrand marries Ebba Gumeer.

1925   Östen Sjöstrand born in Gothenburg on June 16.

1927   His sister Maria born.

1929   His brother Lars-Inge born.

1936   Enters Gothenburg Higher Coeducational School.

1939   Father dies. His estate embezzled by the administrator.

1941   Enters *gymnasium*. Introduced in the home of Hans Pettersson, professor of oceanography.

1945   Growing difficulties of adaptation at home and at school.

1947   Leaves school. Attends lectures at the University of Gothenburg without matriculation. Book reviewer in the *Göteborgs Morgonpost*. Visit to Copenhagen's avant-garde literary circles.

1948   Nervous breakdown and decisive religious crisis. Renewed visit to Copenhagen. Meets authoress Ella Hillbäck.

1949   Marries Ella Hillbäck. Goes to live for some months in Copenhagen. First book of poetry, *Unio*, published.

1950   Joins editorial board of the new literary magazine *Utsikt* (*View*). On a traveling grant from his publisher to London, Paris, and Provence, northern Italy, and Switzerland—together with his wife. Publishes *Consecration*.

1951   Visit to Paris. First meets Gunnar Ekelöf.

1952   Visit to Paris again.

1953   Enters Roman Catholic Church. Publishes *Return*.

1954   Spring and summer in Italy; two months at San Michele, Capri. Stays with Russian-American Futurist poet and painter David Burliuk at Positano. In autumn moves from Gothenburg to permanent residence in Stockholm. Publishes *Spirit and Reality, Essays*, and *Poems between Midnight and Dawn*.

1955   Travels in France and Italy. Publishes *Strange Darkness, Strange Light*.

1956 Tour of Germany and Austria. Moves to apartment in the Stockholm suburb of Vällingby.

1958 Death of brother Lars-Inge. Summer spent on the island Tjörn outside Gothenburg together with composer Sven-Erik Bäck. Writes the opera, *The Banquet*. Publishes *Homelessness and Home*.

1959 Tour of Greece.

1960 Publishes *The World Is Created Every Day: Essays*.

1961 Publishes *The Enigmatic Obstacles*.

1963 Sojourn in Provence. Visit to Norway. Publishes *A Winter in the North*.

1965 In spring to Turkey and Greece; meets Ekelöf in Smyrna, Turkey. In summer rents a chalet in Switzerland.

1966 Long stay in Provence.

1967 Visit to Spain. Publishes *In the Sign of Aquarius*.

1968 Leaves Catholic Church. Visit to Norway. Moves from Stockholm to a house at Mariefred, small town on Lake Mälaren.

1970 Granted Artist's State Pension. Visit to Romania on behalf of the Swedish Radio.

1971 Publishes *The Necessity of Imagination: Essays* and *The Dream is No Façade*.

1972 In spring lecture tour of the U.S.A.

CHAPTER 1

Biographical Sketch

I Family Background and Early Life

"WHEN the morning wind rises and the shadows disperse, this is what I often see: the water shimmering blue and green, and the rock, the warm granite of the West Coast. The solid rock and the moving water—to them I return. I return even though winters, the Swedish winters, the low pressures and the darkness of the soul will hinder me, lock me out (or in). In fact, I know the water and the rock as two basic elements within myself. My dreams prove that this is really so."[1]

With these words Östen Sjöstrand begins an autobiographical essay, thus emphasizing what to him seems most important in his origin and background, the coastal landscape of his native Gothenburg, which to him is also an inner landscape. Rock and water, solid and fluid, stand for a number of antitheses in Sjöstrand's poetic world, for consciousness and the unconscious, for life and death, for intellect and emotional creativity, and many other things. This imagery is firmly rooted in his childhood experience of swimming, sailing, and fishing on summer holidays on the coast or on some small island in the archipelago outside Gothenburg, and it is from this world of light, wind, water, and rock that his poetry derives its freshness and sensuous appeal. The inner meaning of these elements is equally firmly rooted in the immediate experience of the poet, though the relationship between inner and outer reality is a mystery he never stops pondering or trying to evoke poetically. His sense of the reality and fascination of the outer, natural world developed early into an enthusiastic pursuit of physics and natural science, while the equally real and fascinating inner world called for explorations in other, more mystical terms.

The feeling of being a borderer, of having to assert his

15

personal identity in dialectical terms as the sum or synthesis of
two regions or elements, gained support, in the daydreams of
the small boy, from the fact that his surname Sjöstrand literally
means sea-shore, or lake-shore. Surnames derived from nature
are common enough in Sweden, but his particular name took on
far-reaching symbolical dimensions which it retains, at least in
a light-hearted way, in the speculation of the grown-up poet.
His Christian name, by the way, literally means "island-stone"
if it is divided, not quite in accordance with its derivation,
"Ö-sten": one more of these playful childhood associations that
can haunt a poet's mature imagination.

Originally the surname was chosen by Sjöstrand's father for
its poetic qualities. His father's real name was Oscar Pettersson
and he was born in 1884 in a small place in the province of
Småland in the south of Sweden where his father, the poet's
grandfather, owned a farm and a small village store. Oscar
was a person with imagination, and when he abandoned his
parental home, he took his new, poetic name with him in memory
of his humble and idyllic origin on the edge of a small lake.
Though Sjöstrand's father died when the poet was only fourteen
years old, he influenced his son's future development greatly
and not least through the childhood environment he created
for him.

Oscar Sjöstrand came from a province which at the time of
his youth saw many ambitious and energetic young men emigrate
to the United States, and his own life was inspired by the
same pioneering drive, though realized in his own native country.
In his early years, his artistic inclinations dominated. After a
sketchy musical education he opted for a safer future and
entered a training college for teachers and in 1909 he established
himself as schoolmaster in Gothenburg while continuing to
develop his talents as a pianist and violinist to a high level
of amateur performance. He also found other means of giving
some color and excitement to the humdrum life of a schoolmaster: business. One of his brothers had taken up the trade
of book publishing with considerable financial success, and
Oscar Sjöstrand decided to try his luck in the same way. Selling
books by mail order was a new and flourishing trade, and in
the early 1920's he founded a company of his own which

published and sold adventure stories, illustrated magazines, and other forms of light literary entertainment. Some of the publications of the firm were on the risky side—judged by the standards of decorum then prevalent—and the business prospered accordingly. In ten years' time Oscar Sjöstrand was a wealthy man, and although he lost nearly half a million kronor in one day in the early thirties—the blackest day of the Swedish stock exchange—he soon recovered and continued to prosper financially.

It was, then, a well-to-do home into which his son Östen was born in 1925. Oscar Sjöstrand was nearly forty when he met Ebba Larsson Gumeer, a lady fifteen years his junior, born in 1899 as the daughter of a fortification engineer. When she met her future husband about 1920 she was a trained singer of folk songs and romantic *Lieder,* and this accomplishment combined with youthfulness and good looks conquered the enthusiastic, middle-aged bachelor. After their marriage in 1924 music became one of the chief grounds of sympathy and common experience between husband and wife. Among the earliest memories of their children is their mother's singing to the accompaniment of the father on the grand piano, a soft-tuned Blüthner which now dominates the poet's drawing room.

Three children were born in rapid succession. Östen, 1925; Maria, 1927; and Lars-Inge, 1929. In its prosperous days in the thirties the Sjöstrand family afforded a good instance of the way of life of the upper middle class in Gothenburg at that time. Mrs. Sjöstrand was her husband's equal in energy and ambition and she managed her big household with the assistance of a cook, a maid, and various odd hands needed to look after the three residences of the family: the large flat in the center of the town, the villa in the suburb of Askim, and the summer house a little farther south on the coast. In photographs from that time the worthy parents look a solid and respectable bourgeois couple, both rather stout. The atmosphere of the home was anything but philistine, however. Both husband and wife were too eccentric and artistic for that. Members of the family such as Sara, the monkey, and an uncertain number of dogs, cats, and birds, all mentioned in Sjöstrand's autobiographical essay, indicate an unconventional sense of natural life which perhaps was not always considered the best of "form" in bourgeois circles. Of the mother, Sjöstrand writes, "I see mother busy planting, putting twigs and sprigs into the ground and in pots, how everything takes root, brings forth leaves and fruit, vaults of foliage, even indoors."[2]

The guests entertained in the well-to-do house were more often friends of artistic inclination than business people. Regular visitors were members of the Gothenburg Philharmonic Society whom the father joined in the performance of string quartets and piano trios of the traditional Classical and Romantic repertoire: Haydn, Mozart, Beethoven, Schubert, Brahms, among others. Oscar Sjöstrand was very versatile musically, equal to any part and playing the piano, violin, and cello with the same ease. His collection of musical instruments included a Guarneri and a Stradivarius. But it was not only serious, classical music that was heard in his home. His wife loved to sing simple folk songs and popular tunes. Thus music came to be a natural element of life to the children, who used to spend the evenings of chamber music in the drawing-room sofa, rapt in listening, silent and inconspicuous lest the passing of normal bedtime should be noticed. Music has remained a natural element of life to the adult Sjöstrand.

If the origins of Sjöstrand's poetry are to be sought in his childhood environment, we must consider the importance there attached to religion. He has characterized his home as "religiously indifferent," and the baptism and confirmation in the Lutheran State Church meant little more than a concession to conventional behavior. Nevertheless, the father reveals a trait of religious speculation behind the solid façade of the prospering businessman. His choice of subjects to teach after he left his full-time job as schoolmaster is indicative of his private interests: music, drawing, and religion. And those of the books published by his own company that he had written himself show an increasing preoccupation with the ultimate questions of life and death.

Not many books can be attributed to Oscar Sjöstrand with certainty. As early as 1920 he compiled an anonymous anthology, *Swedish Humor,* which is a comprehensive selection of comic verse from various periods. An anthology of a different kind, published in 1937, was likewise prompted more by financial than metaphysical speculation: *The Book of Ghosts. Ghost Stories, First Collection,* published under the pseudonym of C. O. Schöö. No second collection followed, however, in spite of promises to that effect on the last page of the first collection. Instead there appeared in 1938, under the same pseudonym, *Mysteries of Life. From the Secrets of Nature. Tales of Wonderful Events and Experiences, Dreams Come True, and Visions.* A major part of the book is devoted to the teachings of Swedenborg who was of current interest that year because of the celebration of his 250th anniversary.

Oscar Sjöstrand's bent toward religious speculation these years was caused by the illness which ended his life in 1939. Of this his son writes:

My father . . . wintry waves breaking high up on the shore. Only is it *now* that I see those waves. Then, when it happened, the bay of Askim, visible from the tower of our house, was frozen solid to the bottom. I see my father, in the last years of his life: his steps more and more reluctant, how he has to support himself on a bench outside the hospital in Stockholm, the frightening stranger's look as he ascends the steps to our house, says it is no use returning to Stockholm, the cancer cannot be checked. I hear the sounds from the metal box on his right side where the bowels empty. The bed, the bedsores, and the coffin which is carried out, past us.[3]

The deep effects on the boy witnessing this gradual corruption and dying can be felt in a line written nearly thirty years later, "God, grant me not an evil—but a sudden death."[4] Östen was fourteen years old when his father died, and surely that is an early age to be expelled from the paradise of childhood. The metaphor is his own: "It was a kind of life in the Ark, carefree, without sorrows—if our existence was privileged then, this exception was annihilated as if by an earthquake as soon as we believed we trod on solid ground."[5]

The traumatic effect of the death on all the children is even more understandable when the mother's reactions are taken into account. On the advice of well-meaning friends she set out on a round-the-world cruise shortly after the funeral in order to recover from her own loss. The children were left in the care of friends and relatives, and at this crisis the fatherless

boy Östen found himself motherless, too, and in a way responsible
for a smaller sister and brother.

After his mother's return life was full of painful changes. The
house was sold, the animals given away, the town apartment
exchanged for a new one, spacious and respectably situated
but different. The considerable estate of the father would have
afforded his family a carefree existence had the administrator
not been a swindler; his subsequent imprisonment was poor
compensation for the fortune he had embezzled. To these private
straits were added the generally somber and scanty conditions
of the war years.

Oscar Sjöstrand's widow was facing a difficult situation. She
was forty at the time of her bereavement, and after two years
of caring for a mortally sick and disabled husband she felt
entitled to a life of her own and would not give up all prospects
of personal happiness. But her strong sense of propriety and
social convention balked her instinctive attempts to break
through the role of respectable matron. The ensuing psychological conflicts in her own self hardly contributed toward making
her an ideal guide for adolescent children. The difference
between solid appearance and chaotic reality also applied to
her social and financial position. However, she would not
acknowledge the widening gap between the comfortable upper-
middle-class style of living she felt obliged to keep up and her
actual resources. Soon she had to take lodgers in her large
and expensive flat, some of them kind and generous people,
others bitter and disappointed customers who dragged the
children into their own evil circles. The bohemian way of living
in this home where artists, musicians, and diverse lodgers passed
through the rooms and the lives of the children, has been
described vividly and with a sense of picturesque detail in a
novel, *The Circus Wagon,* by a writer who had not experienced
it all at firsthand but who knew it well enough: Östen Sjöstrand's
wife Ella Hillbäck.[6]

The children were not altogether neglected, however, and
they never suffered real want. But it did happen that they ran
out of firewood during the exceptionally cold winters of the
early 1940's so that Östen and his sister had to chop up old
chairs for fuel. It also happened that they had to manage on

tea and biscuits for days, or to buy themselves a cheap meal at a nearby milk bar. These circumstances brought Östen and Maria close together, and with all their childish insecurity and fear they strove as best they could to support each other. They both emerged from these harsh years with a precocious experience of responsibility and with inner wounds which in later life have been liable to open under pressure and plunge both into deep depression. However, their little brother, Lars-Inge, not yet ten years old at the time of his father's death, suffered most in his personal development. Although he could transfer his filial devotion to one of the middle-aged men courting his mother, a Swedish-American painter, he never succeeded in rooting himself in life, and he went through a number of severe inner crises before he was killed (or committed suicide) in a violent car accident in 1959 at the age of 29. His death and burial on a rocky islet in the Gothenburg archipelago are the distressing events that lie behind the poem "The Image of a Helper" in *A Winter in the North*:

I saw the eyes in the stone. Next, feet, a hip
two fingers—people, and fragments of
people. Coming into being. At peace, in travail.

Hands which furiously tore at the rock-wall from within!
Others which drew the stone aside without effort:
enclosing obstacles, a protecting mask, a disguise.[7]

Östen Sjöstrand's life in his late teens shaped itself according to the same pattern as that of countless other artistically and intellectually talented adolescents: beneath a surface of lively social activities and apparently outgoing interests lurked insecurity, anxiety, and desperation. He was expected to show a façade of social adaptation and exerted himself as far as he could. He joined a conservative youth club—his mother was an active member of the Conservative Party—and he did his school work satisfactorily. Between 1936 and 1946 he was a pupil of the Gothenburg Higher Coeducational School, an educationally progressive institution which thrived on the well-to-do bourgeoisie of the town, financially, and spiritually on the idealistic liberal inheritance from the nineteenth-century poet Viktor

Rydberg. During the war years it was administered by Torgny Segerstedt, one of the governors of the school and editor of the influential *Göteborgs Handels- och Sjöfarts-Tidning*. It was he who, in this paper, offered the most passionate and successful resistance to Nazi propaganda and infiltration in Sweden. During the whole of World War II Gothenburg was the stronghold of Anglo-American sympathies and of liberal political ideology. Politically, Östen Sjöstrand is a liberal at heart although recent events on the social and environmental scene have forced him to consider the merits of socialism.

Of decisive importance to his personal and future poetic development was the contact with Hans Pettersson, professor of oceanography and one of the most distinguished scientists of the country, father of a schoolmate of Sjöstrand's who introduced his friend in his home where he was accepted as one of the family. Professor Pettersson was an expansive, romantic, and enthusiastic person well suited to fill a vacuum in the life of the fatherless schoolboy, and the table talk in the Pettersson home, whether in the nearby town apartment or at the summer house close to Bornö Oceanographic Station in the Gullmar Fjord, was welcome food for an avid mind. Hans Pettersson's interests were not confined to narrow academic disciplines. He had embarked on a promising career as a nuclear physicist before he decided to follow in the footsteps of his father, one of Sweden's first oceanographers, and in this field he made several internationally recognized discoveries. He also loved poetry, especially Kipling's, and he was author of many books of popular science and famous for his broadcast lectures on physics and astronomy. And his wife Dagmar, a university graduate in mathematics and science, fully shared her husband's interests and occupations. In their home, cosmology, nuclear fission, and deep-sea sediments were topics of general conversation as common and natural as politics and the events of the day. Here were laid the foundations for Sjöstrand's far-reaching scientific interests which have been growing in range and importance during later years. He is a regular reader of periodicals such as *Nature* and *Scientific American*, and many shelves in his study are occupied by books on physics, biology, and other branches of science.

Within, however, all was chaos. The crises of adolescence and awakening sexuality he had to face and master all by himself, without guidance from any adult of experience, only with his mother's warnings and admonitions reinforcing his own nervousness and vague feelings of guilt. Sjöstrand avoids thinking and talking of these years, but there is no reason to doubt his sister Maria's memories of their struggle for—and against—life: "Everything was in pieces. We were scared, scared, never dared do a thing." Feelings of guilt engendered dreams of purity and romantic fantasies, all pent up: "Östen hardly dared look at a girl." And he had no one to confide in, on these matters, not even in her. She also remembers an actual fit sometime round 1945: Östen beside himself with rage over some of the lodgers, calling them demons, collapsing behind an easy chair, breaking his glasses.

A more severe and drawn-out crisis occurred some time during the summer or autumn of 1947. The mother was away traveling in the United States, Professor Pettersson was away on a tour round the world on board the oceanographic research vessel *Albatross*, and his sister Maria had been admitted to a theater school in Stockholm. So he was lonelier than ever and his distress grew deeper than ever. Since there are no witnesses to tell us exactly what happened we can only guess. Sjöstrand himself cannot stand recalling any details except the turning point in this darkness: a vision of Christ, more irresistibly real than anything else he remembers from that period. What psychic processes accompanied this vision are beyond our reach, but at least we can study their results: from now on Sjöstrand felt sure of his poetic calling.

II *Literary Apprenticeship and Marriage*

The idea of a career in literature did not appear very clearly in Sjöstrand's mind until after his premature departure from school without the certificate necessary for university entrance. Before that he had vaguely dreamt of an academic career in science, but the upsurge of emotional conflicts in 1947 swept aside all plans of a professional education and left art the only alternative, the only means of survival, it seemed to him.

It was no surprising choice considering his parents' musical interests; and his sister and brother were both intent on a future in art: Maria worked as an actress for some years, has spent much time in drawing and painting, and she has also seen a few of her poems in print. Lars-Inge, the younger brother, devoted himself wholeheartedly to painting, and not without success. To Östen, however, poetry was the only branch of art to be seriously considered.

While groping his way toward poetic self-expression, Sjöstrand sought to join the literary circles of Gothenburg, by means of personal contacts and contributions to papers and magazines. From 1947 he wrote regular book reviews for the *Göteborgs Morgonpost* in which he strongly defended the new movement in Swedish poetry and fiction, the School of the Forties, the program of which was a mixture of French Existentialist philosophy and literary modernism in the style of T. S. Eliot, James Joyce, and Franz Kafka. A very favorable review of Axel Liffner's first book of verse, *Opus 0.09*, led to Sjöstrand's acquaintance with the author, and when Liffner became editor of a new literary magazine in Stockholm he readily accepted Sjöstrand's poems and essays for publication and also made him a corresponding member of the editorial staff.[8]

Stockholm was the center of the new school, but in a smaller way Gothenburg could boast a cultural life of its own with a prospering town theater and an active writers' guild that convened in jovial forms under the auspices of a poetically inclined publican. Sjöstrand's friends in this guild helped him in his struggle for recognition and gave him sympathy and personal encouragement, and the tone in which he speaks of them in his autobiographical essay is both tender and nostalgic. No doubt the bright coloring of these memories is to some extent due to the fact that it was there he met his future wife.

His literary horizon at the end of the 1940's was not confined to contemporary Swedish writers, however. He was, and still is, a voracious reader, and plunged himself into the works of the then current authors, *e.g.*, T. S. Eliot, Jean Paul Sartre, Albert Camus, and François Mauriac. As appears from this brief list, he was chiefly concerned with Existentialist or religious writers, as is natural enough in a convinced atheist turned Christian visionary. For up to the crisis of 1947 Sjöstrand, like the majority of educated and "enlightened" Swedes of that day, considered atheism the only intellectually decent creed, and his great vision did not bring about an instant conversion but rather a bewildered search for new spiritual and intellectual bearings. And what writers could be more useful in this search than Existentialists and Catholics of the highest intellectual integrity?

But fortunately there was a contrasting and complementary side to Sjöstrand's personality, light and good-humored, relieving the solemn pathos of his poetic temperament. The young metaphysician was also a boisterous jazz pianist, and not all his reading moved in lofty spiritual regions. For instance, he considerably extended his French vocabulary in the opposite direction by studying the highly naturalistic novel *Voyage au bout de la nuit* by Céline (*i.e.* Louis Destouche), laboriously looking up all the dirty words in a dictionary. Not that Céline's view of life is light, and neither is the short poem of Sjöstrand's celebrating him:

> night spaces
> silence
> like cosmic radiation
> bounded by a solar system
>
> voyageur
> voyageuse
> au bout de la nuit
> night is bounded
> by an outside[9]

An Existentialist sense of the void and of man's loneliness in front of the mysteries of the universe is here combined with images drawn from science—a typical formula in Sjöstrand's early poetry.

Before he could afford to travel in Europe proper Sjöstrand had a foretaste of the Continental literary climate in Denmark, where he first went immediately after the end of the war in the spring of 1945. In 1947 he went to Copenhagen for a shorter stay and in 1949 he spent several months there. On his second

visit he went to see some of the leading Danish authors, Martin
A. Hansen and Viggo Möller among them, and he also struck
up a friendship with the young writer Ole Sarvig. Most of the
writers with whom Sjöstrand consorted in Copenhagen belonged
to the so-called Heretical Group, *i.e.* the group behind the new
literary magazine *Heretica*. Its first issue appeared early in 1948
and as is often the case with new reviews it attracted a number
of young experimenting poets and novelists without definite
artistic affiliations. *Heretica* did not open with a manifesto or
program but some conception of the aims of its editors can be
formed by studying the sober advertisement (printed on the
back of the first issue) for the general products of the small
publishing firm responsible for the magazine:

The publishers will concentrate on bringing out important and
typical works of criticism in the fields of the fine arts, philosophy, and
history. Without editorial bias in favor of a one-sided approach to
the present cultural situation, yet one aspect is given precedence
before all others: that of the artist. Today the artist, the poet, is, as
long as he thinks as artist and poet, the most valid representative
of man in cultural society because his thinking is exclusively based on
personal experience, not on professional or political allegiances.

The poet, that is to say, does occupy a place at the center of
the social life of his time, but his creative work is granted
independence by means of its personal integrity. With a slight
shift of stress, natural for one who has not yet embarked upon
his own literary career, Sjöstrand gives a similar picture of the
contemporary Swedish literary scene in one of his first contributions to the *Göteborgs Morgonpost*: "The chief concern of the
young generation has been to find a credible view of life. The
poet of today is as much philosopher as maker of poems."[10]
Problems of *Weltanschauung* were given ample space in *Heretica*
during the six years of its existence. They had not been neglected
by the School of the Forties either, but in Copenhagen Sjöstrand
encountered a more tolerant and informed attitude toward Christianity and the possibilities of Christian art. Small wonder then
that he found the Heretics a stimulating environment, and a
complete set of their magazine still occupies a place of honor
in his library. His gratitude for the spiritual hospitality of the

Danes he expressed publicly in giving his second book the Danish-sounding title, *Invigelse* (*Consecration*).

Along with his literary and journalistic apprenticeship he conducted a restless search for a religious frame that could encompass the vision he treasured within himself. The cool State Church piety he had met as a boy had no place for private divine apparitions, nor any answers to personal problems. The current fashion for Neo-Thomist philosophy and theology, on the other hand, seemed to afford a more adequate framework, and Sjöstrand embarked upon a course of Catholic reading and approached the priests of the Roman Catholic congregation in Gothenburg. Guided by them he found a doctrine of acceptable intellectual standards which, he thought, allowed space for personal mysticism. He also found a tempting means of liberation from the burden of guilt that perpetually weighed upon him.

Highly favorable to this development was his acquaintance with an attractive member of the writers' guild in Gothenburg, the poet and writer Ella Hillbäck, who was already approaching the Roman Church. With her wider experience of life—she is his senior by ten years—her warm and generous personality, her religious faith and literary position, she offered Sjöstrand the refuge and support he so badly needed, and in September, 1949, the couple were quietly married. A slightly romantic account of the circumstances accompanying the wedding is to be found in her aforementioned novel, *The Circus Wagon*. The newly-wed couple had a small apartment of their own in Gothenburg but went to spend the first months of their married life in Copenhagen. Reflections of the fullness of their love are to be found in much of Ella Hillbäck's poetry, particularly in the love songs published in *I denna skog* (*In This Wood*, 1953).

That was the end of a long and painful adolescence. His loneliness was broken, he had taken his spiritual bearings, and his belief in a poetic calling was confirmed.

Husband and wife decided to devote themselves wholeheartedly to literature. Sjöstrand sacrificed the financial security obtained from working as a bank clerk—as did his admired predecessor T. S. Eliot, whom he had met in Gothenburg the year before. From the first day of their married life both Ella Hillbäck and Östen Sjöstrand have relied solely on their writing, with a budget never stretching beyond the next month. Growing recognition has meant growing material security over the years, mainly through private patronage and government grants, but even at its best the vocation of a poet in Sweden (as elsewhere) is a hazardous career. In the early days this hand-to-mouth style of living held its special charms of bohemian independence. Keen travelers, the couple often spent all their cash on third-class railway tickets for the Continent, went away to Paris or Provence or Italy, sending articles and poems to papers and magazines back home, eagerly waiting for their small fees to be mailed down to them in time for paying the modest hotel bills. Having children was out of the question at this stage, and when they became more settled the hope was never fulfilled. Traveling together in foreign countries, meeting hardships and unexpected happiness together but with no family to share it, they became very close.

III   *Thomism and Mysticism*

Sjöstrand's first book of poetry appeared in 1949 under the title of *Unio* (or *unio*, to be exact; it was the fashion then to avoid capital letters altogether in poetry). The title has a double meaning. On the one hand, it refers to the longed for, dreamt of, and finally achieved blissful union with another person in love; and on the other, to *unio mystica*, the union with the divine in religious contemplation. This twofold union contains an antinomy, however, between human and divine love, between this world and a transcendent world, which Sjöstrand hoped to resolve with the aid of Thomist theology. According to St Thomas Aquinas and his modern interpreters, the world is related to God through a system of universal analogies. It is not only in religious contemplation that man gains knowledge of God but also through the revelations of natural creation. In consequence, it is the duty of the Christian poet to explore and express both these roads to divine knowledge, the inner, abstract road and the one that leads through the analogies of the created world. The ultimate goal of both is *unio*.

This search for knowledge of his own identity is sometimes

expressed in terms reminiscent of the well-known antithesis between potentiality and actuality in the philosophy of Aristotle, on which St. Thomas built his system:

> a boundless access between
> possibility and truth
> shall be mine
> and I shall be
> a burning vertigo
> in the dreamless spaces of Space[11]

Sometimes we find more direct references to Thomist terminology, as in the dichotomy in the following lines:

> man and thing
> existence and essence:
> eyelids closed
> round a burning sail[12]

The imagery employed to express the ecstatic and visionary states of mind in *Unio* is often airy and elusive but does not altogether lack sensuous elements. Ocean, wind, sails, sunlight reflected in water, are images that recur throughout Sjöstrand's work and they are introduced here in a tone of vibrating intensity and dazzling purity which almost make the reader welcome the relief of a set of somewhat more earthy prose poems.

Among the literary influences noticeable in *Unio*, the ecstatic diction of Erik Lindegren's *Suites* (1947) is most in evidence, and behind him looms the whole Modernist and Symbolist tradition, with which Sjöstrand was busy familiarizing himself. Scattered allusions such as the drunken boat in piece No. 28 point to Rimbaud, the prose poems are descendants of Baudelaire's *Poèmes en prose*, and the book closes with a quotation from Charles Vildrac—to mention only a few instances. The compact imagery and the sometimes baffling metaphors together with the Existentialist sense of the threat of nothingness and the void, are traits that *Unio* has in common with Swedish poetry of the 1940's generally.

Allowing for the literary reminiscences inevitable in a writer's first book, *Unio* has a unity of tone and theme that is unique in

Sjöstrand's work. It is the shy and naked confession of "the awful daring of a moment's surrender," made by a youth fervent in spirit. Water and wind, stars and space, are recurrent images, but the poet has not lost himself in the elemental depths of the universe but found his true self there.

Consecration (1950) is a direct continuation of Unio but it is richer and more varied in content. Formally it is more unified, however. The long introductory poem, "Madonna of the Plague," ("Pestjungfru") is written in a kind of unrhymed triplet which is the modernist's version of Dante's terza rima. The rest of the book is made up of small miniature pieces consisting of a triplet followed by a couplet. In "Madonna of the Plague" Sjöstrand turns from cosmic infinity to the want and suffering of this world. The theme is purification and atonement and the poetic pattern derives from Divina Commedia and from T. S. Eliot's Ash Wednesday.[13] Probably Albert Camus's novel La Peste influenced the motif of the plague—the closed city and the burning summer sun appear in the very first stanzas. And as with Camus, there are numerous references to the Second World War, though without the allegorical disguise of the novel. It is one of the longest poems in all of Sjöstrand's work but also the one in the first two collections that as a whole gives the strongest impression of literary exercise. The short pieces in Consecration are more genuine. In imagery and tone they form a direct continuation of Unio. Water, wind, air, and space are still dominant themes, and there are several explicit references to Scholasticism and Christian mysticism. One motto is culled from St. Thomas, another from Meister Eckhart. New, however, are the allusions to science, especially oceanography, which give substance to the otherwise more vaguely conceived elemental symbolism. Other allusions point to musical inspiration, Debussy in the first place, and the importance of music to Sjöstrand's creative work cannot be too strongly emphasized. The place of music and science in his work will be considered at some length in Chapters Two and Three.

Both Unio and Consecration were well received by leading critics who praised their "genuine lyrical radiance"[14] and forecast a promising future for the young poet. Most of them also drew attention to the Catholic Christian qualities of the books, and the essays Sjöstrand published at this time in various reviews confirmed the general opinion of him as a Catholic writer. Some of these essays were reprinted in a collection of prose pieces, *Spirit and Reality* (1954), which illustrates the typical admiration of Swedish converts of that day for the intellectual clarity and spiritual depth of the French Catholic writers. Pierre Jean Jouve, Pierre Emmanuel, Jean Cayrol, François Mauriac, and Georges Bernanos were among the great discoveries in his reading during these years, and personal visits to some of them and to the great cathedrals of France strengthened his faith and enthusiasm.

Perhaps a word should be said here about Sjöstrand's reading in general. As a self-taught man with an immense respect for learning, he has set himself, and fulfilled, extremely ambitious courses of reading in many different fields, such as theology, philosophy, history, music, physics, biology, psychology, and of course poetry and fiction. With a solid grounding in English, German, and French from school and a natural gift for languages, he is fluent in these three. Italian offers him no difficulties, he has a smattering of Latin and has even picked up some modern Greek during his visits to that country. This comprehensive linguistic ability together with an insatiable appetite for books makes it difficult to give an exact description of his reading, especially since his own collection of books does not contain more than a fragment of what he has read: he has always depended very much on libraries and not shunned vast institutions such as the Royal Library in Stockholm or the Bibliothèque Nationale in Paris.

Voracious reading of this kind, wholly unrestrained by academic discipline, is not exceptional among creative writers, but invariably leads to highly personal interpretations and combinations of the matters absorbed. That an author has made a deep impression on Sjöstrand does not necessarily mean that this author has been assimilated into an ordered body of learning but rather that the ideas set forth by him have activated deeply emotional, creative patterns within the poet. As general observations these are of course commonplace, but it would be well to keep them in mind when considering Sjöstrand's indebtedness to Roman Catholic writers. It would be easy to make out a case for

comprehensive influences from them based on the evidence of
numerous articles and essays in which Sjöstrand extols his Catholic masters and points out the intellectual structure of their
faith. However, it was not so much a matter of his being per-
suaded by intellectual arguments as of his seeking such arguments in order to justify the emotional acceptance of a faith
which seemed the best solution to his personal problems. Of
course he did not himself consider his conversion in these
terms at the time, but the fact that his subsequent departure
from that same faith was dictated by emotional incompatibility
and not by any doubts as to the validity of Thomist philosophy,
confirms the impression that he approached that faith on the
same grounds in the first place. During the early years of his
new religious life, however, he was very seriously concerned
with the theological aspects of Catholicism and gladly entered
upon the course of doctrinal instruction prescribed for every
convert prior to his actual acceptance into the Church, which
did not take place until 1953. He was even nicknamed Thomas
among his friends after the "angelic doctor."

It was not only the right way of thinking that concerned him
but the right way of living and pursuing his poetic calling.
And in these matters he sought guidance from another Thomas,
the author of *Imitatio Christi*. The following extracts from a
diary he kept about 1950 show how closely interwoven were
the religious and the poetic ideas in his everyday thought. For
instance these observations of July 25, 1951:

It is not a matter of finding the right words. In fortunate cases that
means epitomizing the holiness of life in especially favored moments,
with all that this generally implies: defending life without conviction;
believing that it matters only to others, that you yourself are not
among the living. You cannot set out to find words for the use of
others. And you betray life by not pleading your own cause—as well
as by refraining from pleading.

"Go and sit down in the lowest room and thou shalt be bidden to
go up higher, for that which is exalted cannot prevail without that
which is abased" (Thomas à Kempis). . . . In *Imitatio Christi* I think
I have discovered for the first time the meaning of a "book of edification." It is the opposite of literature. You are not "influenced" by a
book of edification, you recognize yourself in it.

Obviously Sjöstrand tended to put religion above poetry; so much so, in fact, that he believed to have done with poetry altogether. The title of his second book of verse, *Consecration*, not only refers to the poet's calling as poet, but implied a consecration to the silence of a divine life beyond poetry, and he honestly believed that he had fulfilled his poetic mission and was now facing the task of building a new life on purely spiritual foundations without creative art as a means of sustenance, either literally or psychologically. What Sjöstrand was actually doing in drawing these extreme consequences of his new faith was to put that faith to the test. Could it save his inner life? Heal the wounds and resolve the conflicts that had tortured him ever since he entered adolescence? The test failed, and Sjöstrand returned to poetry. And the title of his next book was *Return* (1953).

This return may be interpreted in different ways. It may be seen as a sobering-up after a bout of spiritual intoxication, and also as an adjustment to current trends in Swedish literature. The warm critical response to *Unio* and *Consecration* had fostered dreams in Sjöstrand of inaugurating a new Christian era in contemporary poetry but literary developments in Sweden during the 1950's turned in different directions, toward homely realism and experiments in Concretism. But even if Sjöstrand set out to acquire an entirely new style in *Return*, it would be a false simplification to explain it solely in terms of contemporary literary trends.

Instead, we may choose to explain his poetic return in the terms adopted by himself in the collection of essays, *Spirit and Reality*. Alluding to the opening motif of T. S. Eliot's *Ash Wednesday*, "Because I do not hope to turn again," he maintains that this poem "belongs in the first place to those who recognize the greater problem in the return to man, to that in man which is more himself than he is himself. In the final analysis *Ash Wednesday* is a poem of return, an esthetic affirmation of life on the basis of nothingness, opening up toward the Christian faith."[15] Sjöstrand's critical prose is not always as clear as might be wished, but it seems that the passage quoted has a more immediate bearing on his own situation than on Eliot's poem. It seems to indicate esthetic grounds for his own return to poetry

which entail no breach with the religious belief of his first
two books. The same idea is central to the first essay in *Spirit
and Reality*, "Poetry and Mysticism." Mysticism, it is there
maintained, is of its essence silence, while the essence of
poetry is words:

The mystic begins by refuting that which is most important in art,
namely the senses, or rather the evidence of the senses. Not that art
is failed mysticism. To the mystic, words are an accident, violently
breaking the clear glass of silence, like an octopus darkening the
transparent, sunlit water. With the poet it is altogether different. To
him, words are a condition of life. Having to utter them may be
painful, to himself and to others, he knows that; they may tear open
old wounds. Words may be obstacles to him; the right, the true
words may elude him. But silence is not his last refuge (even if it
may seem so to him at times). Silence is the painful isolation, the pause
for recuperation necessary to renewed vision and creativity.[16]

If we are to believe these essays, Sjöstrand's way from *Consecration* to *Return,* through silence back to art, was a piece of
personally experienced spiritual and esthetic dialectics. But
surely other forces were operating, too, the origin and direction
of which he can hardly have recognized at the time. The des-
perate and chaotic position from which Sjöstrand had been
rescued through the three decisive events of the late 1940's—his
vision of Christ and the theological superstructure built on it,
his marriage, and his first success as a poet—this position remained unresolved. He fell victim to renewed depressions,
anxiety and feelings of guilt. In the same entry of the diary
quoted above he also wrote:

This is my experience: The price we have to pay for good will—is
anguish. (Perhaps I should use a weaker word than anguish; that is
a word for the night, not what confronts me in broad daylight. Nevertheless, anguish is the right word.) Good will—it always demands that
we be prepared to face our past in a spirit of contrition. It is not so
much a question of "departure," but rather of keeping a vigil, in good
will, of bygone years. How many of us reach as far as the utter
darkness where the wounds of the past are healed and where the
cries of hidden pain no longer outvoice the silence?

One explanation for his return is that Sjöstrand simply needed poetic creativity in order to master his life and keep in mental health. Neither theology nor mysticism was the answer to his personal problems. Returning to poetry in 1953, the same year as he entered the Roman Catholic Church, was in fact his first step away from that church although he did not recognize it then. His most fervently Catholic book appeared the year after, *Poems Between Midnight and Dawn* (1954), a slender volume exquisitely turned out in a private edition of a few hundred numbered copies. It was dedicated to Pierre Jean Jouve, the French poet, convert—and heretic—who entitled one of his books *Symphony to God.*

IV   *Return and Departure*

The poetic world to which Sjöstrand made his return in 1953 is very different from the ethereal universe of his preceding books. The seascapes and visions from outer space in these were also states of mind and metaphysical approximations, and the only connection they have with actual places and environments is oblique: the imagery of water, wind, and sails evoke the poet's west coast background. *Return,* on the other hand, is overtly connected with definite places and more concerned with outward reality. One poem is entitled "The Montparnasse Churchyard," another "Route—Ile de France," and the suite "Province" deals with Gothenburg and its hinterland. The literary references are no longer restricted to the Catholic tradition. For instance, the early nineteenth-century Swedish poet Erik Johan Stagnelius is pictured and paraphrased, Strindberg is invoked, and one piece is dedicated to Sjöstrand's contemporary, Gunnar Ekelöf. These are all outward signs of an inner reorientation, of an attempt to build a new poetic world and a new language and style. And what he attempted here, he did not fully achieve until some ten years later.

The reorientation inaugurated in *Return* was brought to its practical consequences in the following year. The circle of writers and artists in Gothenburg to which Sjöstrand and his wife belonged was breaking up, and anyway Gothenburg was beginning to feel rather narrow; besides the financial opportunities there were becoming insufficient. So when the couple came home from an extended sojourn in Italy in the spring and summer of 1954, they decided to move to Stockholm, the center of literary life in Sweden. Settling there meant personal contacts with publishers and editors and hence better opportunities of earning from their writing.

There was another source of employment and income in Stockholm: The Swedish Broadcasting Company. Sjöstrand soon became a regular contributor there of poetic readings and talks and discussions on literary topics. More important to his own development was his connection with the Broadcasting Company's department of music. After his immersion in Debussy and Impressionist music generally, he was now seeking creative stimulation in contemporary music, and it appeared that he could be useful in helping to introduce such music to a wider audience. He well knew that settling in Stockholm meant settling in a center of avant-garde music, and that was one of the reasons for moving there.

The great problem of avant-garde music is of course its lack of an audience outside a small circle of professionals and other enthusiasts. Whether scoring for a traditional symphony orchestra or an electronic outfit, modern composers are painfully aware of the costs of producing their works which, with no eager public to pay, means that they have to rely on official patronage. During the last two decades the Swedish Broadcasting Company has extended its patronage to a great number of young composers, having their works performed at public broadcast concerts, providing ample broadcasting time for discussions, and even publishing a monthly magazine for running comments on the contemporary musical scene, *Contemporary Music*. Due to this encouragement and to a new anti-academic attitude in the Royal Academy of Music, Stockholm may be looked upon, in the 1950's and 1960's, as a center of considerable prestige in the international world of music.

Sjöstrand's contacts with this musical life meant not only opportunities of work, self-education, creative stimulation, and personal acquaintance with composers, performing artists and critics—it also influenced his attitude to his own writing. As a reaction against the Modernist esotericism of the School of the

Forties, during the fifties and sixties there was a general feeling that the creative writer should step out of the ivory tower and concern himself with everyday realities, even get politically involved. It may be argued that this entailed considerable dangers to artistic integrity. At least Sjöstrand would have none of it, and the ensuing threat of isolation from leading literary circles was easier to bear in so far as he could find sympathy and support among avant-garde musicians, for whom a certain esotericism is unavoidable. With them he also shared the conviction that the creative artist better serves society and mankind by pursuing his art in uncompromising obedience to its requirements than by attempting directly to influence the social and political development of his time. And this conviction Sjöstrand has vindicated in his later poetry where he reveals long-standing insights into the real dilemma facing modern society—insights which have only just begun to dawn upon those whose vision has been limited to the conventional sociopolitical perspectives.

If Sjöstrand was isolated to some extent from his fellow writers in Stockholm, owing partly to his literary and partly to his religious creed, that did not exclude personal contacts. It was during his first years in Stockholm that he became personally acquainted with Gunnar Ekelöf (1907–1968), the outstanding Swedish poet of this century. It was an acquaintance that developed into a friendship based on a precarious equilibrium of common interests and antagonistic views of life. For one thing their family backgrounds bore striking similarities. Both fathers were of lower-middle-class Småland origins, had climbed to a position of considerable wealth in Gothenburg and Stockholm respectively, and had died when their sons were still mere boys. The estates of both were subsequently obliterated, leaving the sons to accommodate their bourgeois tastes and habits to an enforced bohemianism as best they could. The complex relationships to the mothers of these fatherless adolescents in both cases underwent painful developments exposing them to grave psychic disturbances in later life. Gunnar Ekelöf was an arrogant and passionate person of great intellectual superiority, a neurotic (for what the word is worth), and an incorrigible "outsider" in all human affairs.

The similarities of their backgrounds was something that

Sjöstrand discovered only gradually. He first responded to the authority of the twenty years older man and writer of undisputed genius, and did at times succumb to—unconscious—imitation of him. Among their common interests were music, French literature, Oriental mysticism, food, and the eighteenth-century style of life as reflected in memoirs of that time and in Rococo art and architecture. But on one vital point they could not agree. Ekelöf, though in fact a deeply religious person and poet, was an inveterate blasphemer and a passionate antagonist of everything Christian. This blunt opposition in matters of faith was no obstacle to their friendship, however, not until the last year of Ekelöf's life when he was far gone in mortal illness and uninhibited aggression on his side caused estrangement between the former friends. The difference in religious opinions also safeguarded Sjöstrand's sense of spiritual independence, though Ekelöf's influence may have contributed to his gradual retreat from Rome.

It is difficult to sum up Sjöstrand's literary indebtedness to Ekelöf in a few words. It is mainly a matter of poetic diction that would require extensive exemplification to be clearly grasped. Generally, Ekelöf reinforced Sjöstrand's preoccupation with the music of poetry and with the possibilities of giving verbal expression to transcendent insights. A point, besides Christianity, where they differed was the importance and role of science in the arts and humanities. Ekelöf was a typical exponent of the "two cultures" attitude, only that he rather inclined to deny the cultural claims of science altogether. Sjöstrand on the other hand became increasingly absorbed in the problem of integrating science, humanities, and the arts in a new totality.

His first collection of poems to be published after the removal to Stockholm was *Strange Darkness, Strange Light* (1955), which contains a series of lyrical "post cards": "From Ravenna," "From Rome," "From the Mediterranean," and so on. "Father Damien" is interesting in hinting at an incipient shift in Sjöstrand's Catholic involvement from the problems of doctrine and personal salvation to those of the social responsibilities of a Christian. The sense of universal brotherhood and compassion with those who suffer oppression is given almost Expressionist intensity in "For Those at the Limit":

For you outcast in darkness
for you forced to keep silence
in this desert of oppressed and exiled lives
for you with broken driving belts
with the wheels of emotion worn out
for you who can no longer wait for day
because day has changed into boundlessness
for you in the searchlight world of catchwords
where fear with a movement of the hand can extinguish
all the stars in everyone
for you comrades among watching eyes
tormented by the dark's denied questions
this song under the earth
this last that is possible
the most secret crime
the only thing possible—like a seed,
like a flower,
like the mining town's dark brown rain.[17]

Sjöstrand remained in Stockholm for fourteen years—fourteen outwardly uneventful years, save travels abroad, intermittent psychic crises, and one great shock, the death in a car accident of his younger brother Lars-Inge, mentioned above. The traumatic effect of this death was not only due to its suddenness and cruelty but to the feelings of guilt it engendered, which plunged Sjöstrand into deep depression. Inwardly, the Stockholm years meant radical changes, both progressive and regressive; regression to the fundamentals of his spiritual and creative life beneath the laboriously erected dogmatic superstructure, and a progression toward a new vision, a new faith, toward a synthesis of all the strains in his life and work. The breakthrough to this new vision is not manifest until *In the Sign of Aquarius* (1967) but the preceding collections of poetry form preliminary statements of increasing authority—besides, of course, containing many self-sufficing texts.

One aspect of Sjöstrand's return to poetry was the acceptance of this world as the home of man, while the mystic in him still tended to regard the business of life on earth as a pilgrimage to far countries beyond the horizon. This ambivalence is reflected already in the title of the 1958 collection, *Homelessness and Home*. On the affirmative side it contains such delightful pieces

as "In Praise of Deciduous Trees" and "Swedish Summer Forest,"
while "Homecoming" speaks of crossing frontiers not to be
found on any earthly maps. The ambivalence is not a static antithesis, however, but a dialectic pattern of repeated acts and
experiences. In the poem "Return" the feeling of homelessness
is described as an alienation from life caused by Sjöstrand's
invisible enemy, the nocturnal anguish. The "thoughts of sleep-
lessness" tell him one and the same thing over and over again:
"That which is mine, is only a tomb"; but suddenly, like a sub-
terranean wave of fresh water, there is "the *other* voice," full
of hope and promise.

> Two voices. Two kingdoms.
> In a no man's land, in a fifth quarter
> in between:
> the witness that is me,
> the choice that is mine[18]

Awakening to the "other voice" is like a perpetual homecoming
from the lonely despair of the night. But even when at home
in the world of sunlight on green foliage and running water,
he retains the memories of the night, always a borderer between
two kingdoms. The emphasis on the free choice in the lines
quoted shows that Sjöstrand still interpreted his situation in
Existentialist terms, but in spite of the perhaps divine "thou"
of the subsequent part of the poem, the whole feeling of it
smacks more of the secular blend of Existentialism than, say,
Jacques Maritain's abstruse synthesis of Thomas Aquinas and
Bergson. Nevertheless, the book *Homelessness and Home* ends
on an unmistakably Christian note:

> ... qui pro Christi nomine sanguinem suum fudit
> Oh focus that gathers the scattered light!

Sjöstrand's next book is a collection of essays, *The World Is
Created Every Day* (1960), containing a miscellany of reprints
treating poets such as Salvatore Quasimodo, René Char, and
Norman Nicholson and novelists such as G. K. Chesterton, Evelyn
Waugh, François Mauriac, Graham Greene, and Georges Ber-

nanos, their work being brought together under the title "Does the 'Catholic Novel' Exist?" The most interesting of the essays is, however, devoted to more general reflections on the art of poetry, "Have Words Lost Their Meaning in Our Time?" It might be described as a sermon on a text from T. S. Eliot's "Burnt Norton":

> Words strain,
> Crack and sometimes break, under the burden,
> Under the tension, slip, slide, perish,
> Decay with imprecision, will not stay in place,
> Will not stay still. Shrieking voices
> Scolding, mocking, or merely chattering,
> Always assail them. The Word in the desert
> Is most attacked by voices of temptation . . .

In his exegesis of these lines Sjöstrand expresses his deep concern with the misuse of words in modern society, the violation of them in journalistic jargon and political propaganda. Behind this decay of language he perceives a general decay of human communication reflected in the verbal disintegration of much contemporary literature. The feeling of the inadequacy of language to express man's most important experiences he recognizes as an eternal phenomenon, intensified during periods of cultural transition such as ours, and always present in times of war when man stands face to face with destruction and death. Yet, Sjöstrand goes on to say,

it seems as if the modern crisis of language was more profound than ever before. . . . The knowledge that there are nuclear bombs each capable of many times the destructive energy used altogether during the last World War—that knowledge is already threatening to reduce language to a scrap heap. But perhaps emptiness has always been boundless, and where are the manometers to gauge the pressure of nothingness throughout the ages? With many mystics we feel that their experience of the dark night of the soul would not have been greater or very much different, had they been living today. But perhaps more people feel the threat of nothingness these days; it is not only the poets who are inwardly paralyzed by the phantoms of destruction—

For myself, the temptation to resign has been epitomized in one voice and one situation. I hear Hölderlin's weary words at the frontier of silence, "Die Sprache ist ein grosser Überfluss" (Language is a great superfluity)—or I think of the dying Constantine Cavafy, the Greek poet, a sheet of paper in his hand, with something written on it, but just this: a full stop and round about it, for the sake of emphasis, a circle.

Still we all know: the language of communication and fellowship is needed now more than ever.

. . . .

In principle I think the situation can be considered as the relationship of the poet to the mystic. It needs to be said again and again: the kind of poetry which according to Mallarmé attains perfection in the empty, white sheet of paper, is the defeat of poetry. The poet's road to reality leads through words. The goal of the mystic is wordless silence.[19]

The burden of the argument is the same as in the earlier essay on "Poetry and Mysticism" but with one difference. Ten years earlier Sjöstrand had chosen words instead of silence, overtly for the sake of poetry as such, in fact for the sake of his own personal needs. Now, in 1960, his allegiance to words is dictated by his concern for something more fundamental, for humanity and the urgent need of renewed communication between men.

The problem of language is dominant in his next book of poetry, *The Enigmatic Obstacles* (1961). The obstacles referred to are language itself: "Language hinders me / Words bind me."[20] But just as Eliot contrasts words with the Word, so Sjöstrand contrasts the conception of language as an obstacle with "the Creative Word."[21]

All Sjöstrand's books contain documents of inner crises, and *A Winter in the North* (1963) often speaks of depression, anxiety, longing for rebirth and renewed life. A small selection of lines and phrases from different poems in this book will indicate the poet's frame of mind:

A wall, an impassable, impenetrable wall.[22]

My God, my God
What is happening in this night?[23]

Nothing more could be taken from me. I knew who I was.
But only then did I fathom the full extent to which it
was once more a winter in the North.[24]

I thought, How shall man ever regain his wings?[25]

Much of this depression and hopeless yearning for something
new is no doubt a reflection of Sjöstrand's personal feelings at
the time following his brother's death. But he also felt his
depression and sterility as a reflection of the state of the society
in which he lived. The aimless futility of modern metropolitan
life has been given well-known expression by T. S. Eliot in the
image of London's underground railway,[26] and Sjöstrand uses
the same kind of image to much the same effect in *A Winter
in the North*. The train that beats against "its metalled ways"
in his poem is the suburban line connecting his Vällingby with
central Stockholm. The rattling of these trains forms a recurrent
motif in "The Dark Season," accompanying thoughts of hopelessness and feelings of time lost and unredeemed.

But in this darkness of cold and winter there are also hopes
and signs of light and spring. In poems and prose pieces that
seem—and often are—direct transcriptions of dreams or hallu-
cinatory visions, a new reality emerges. Winter is not only the
season of death but of the hibernating seeds of life. As in the
last two sections of "Outflows":

II
The solitary grain—
The quiet embers—

And the fire leaps through the veins
lights up the cranium, head, shoulders:

the light breaks up in crystals
till she sees,

on the other side of the fragile alabaster wall:
the shadow, her namesake;

freed from the turning wheel,
freed from destruction, despair,

she dances with raised hands,
and hails the liberator, the sun!

III
The coach driver—
harnessing two red mares,
holding them in firm gentle reins—

when they glide forward quietly
in the damp warm night,
through the mists.

Hoof-beats?
No, the moss softly yielding
under their hooves.

And their muzzles, lowered in self-forgetfulness
towards the cave where the green germinates
before spring.[27]

An important aspect of the frosty depression that weighed so
heavily on Sjöstrand during these years is his relationship to
the Catholic faith. It was not so much the fact that he became
isolated from many of his fellow writers in Stockholm because
of this faith—at times he even felt ostracized because of it.
Much worse were his own doubts, his growing awareness of the
inadequacy of the Christian doctrine of the soul and his increasing impatience with the Church's failure to meet the social
challenges of the modern world. Indications of a social commitment in his poetry after *Return* have already been mentioned, and as Sjöstrand gradually moves out of the wintry
season of the early 1960's this commitment becomes a dominant
feature of his work. The much regretted failure of the Pope
to accept the necessity of contraception in order to safeguard
the future of humankind appeared to Sjöstrand, as it did to so
many other faithful Christians, not only unhappy and mis-
guided but outright cynical. Nor is this the only point where
the Roman Catholic Church has lately antagonized responsible
Christians in their sense of social decency and human fellowship. A book which deeply affected Sjöstrand was *A Question
of Conscience* (1967) by the rebellious scholar and priest
Charles Davis.

Perhaps this estrangement from the Church on grounds of social conscience would not have occurred had not Sjöstrand come to doubt vital points in the Catholic doctrine. As we have seen, he eagerly embraced this doctrine as a means of ordering and mastering his confused and guilt-ridden inner life and as an intellectual framework for his private vision of Christ. But as the years went by it became more obvious that his inner conflicts had not been resolved by his faith, and as for visions he had more of them, not of divine presence perhaps, but in dreams and agitated states of mind he confronted an inner, psychic reality which orthodox Christianity did not seem to have room for. The Christian doctrine more and more appeared as only one of many possible constructions to be put on the experiences of the human psyche, and one which disqualified itself by its claims to possess the exclusive, unique truth.

In his search for other ways of interpreting his inner experience Sjöstrand naturally inclined toward the other great tradition running parallel with the orthodox Christian one: the Gnostic, occult, or Romantic tradition, whatever one prefers to call it, the tradition that grants man the possibility of union with God and the whole of creation through descending into the depths of his own self. One version of this tradition Sjöstrand encountered in Indian religion and philosophy. For instance, the "turning wheel" in the poem "Outflows" just quoted is an obvious reference to the Buddhist doctrine of metempsychosis, and evidence of his interest in Eastern wisdom is also found in *The World Is Created Every Day*, in an essay called "Buddha and the Western World."

To take another clue from "Outflows," the phrase "the shadow, her namesake" points to Carl Gustaf Jung's version of depth psychology. In fact Jung, and psychologists and theologians influenced by him, played an important part in shattering the Thomist crust that covered his dynamic and rebellious depths. As we shall see later, Jungian ideas permeate Sjöstrand's poetry in many ways, but with regard to religion two aspects seem of special importance. The first one is Jung's insistence upon the darkness, the shadow, as an integral part of the complete "individuated" personality, a view which overturns traditional Christian conceptions of good and evil and robs the problem of personal guilt of its absolute consequences in salvation or damnation. The motto of Sjöstrand's latest book of poetry, *The Dream is No Façade,* should be seen in this context: "Bury your guilt and dig up your intelligence" (Wesker). Secondly, Jung's analysis of religious symbolism revealed to Sjöstrand psychological contents common to most religions and hence invalidated the Christian claim to build on a unique revelation superior to any other. Among the Jungian writers who besides the master meant most to Sjöstrand in his liberation from Catholic authority were two believing Catholics— priests, in fact: the French psychoanalyst Ignace Lepp, author of *Psychanalyse de l'Athéisme* (1961) and *La Mort et ses Mystères: Approches psychanalytique* (1966), and Victor White with his *Soul and Psyche* (1960).

The fundamental ideas of Jungian psychology are not new, of course, but can be found at least implicit in the writings of many mystics and, metaphysically elaborated, in the Romantic movement. And Sjöstrand had access to both these sources. His interest in, for instance, Meister Eckhart has already been mentioned, and the Romantic view of the soul and the universe was outlined for him at school in the study of nineteenth-century Swedish literature. The Swedish Romantic poets to impress him most were Stagnelius, Atterbom, and Rydberg—the last-named a kind of patron saint of Sjöstrand's school. After leaving school he took a deeper plunge into the profound waters of Romanticism by reading Albert Béguin's comprehensive study *L'Ame Romantique, Essai sur le Romantisme Allemand et la Poésie Française* (ed. of 1946), in which dream and its sources in the unconscious are made the central theme of Romanticism. Béguin also brings home the twofold aspect of the unconscious: on the one hand, a dimension of the human psyche, and on the other, a dimension of nature in general. And according to many mystics, Romantics and Jungians alike, at the bottom of his unconscious soul man is one with the universe; there microcosm and macrocosm meet, just as in Indian philosophy the essence of the self, Atman, is one with the totality of existence, Brahman.

The mystic doctrine of correspondence has a very real meaning to Sjöstrand, and as we shall see he thinks he has found it embraced, in a different language, by some of the most advanced among modern physicists. This explains how his studies in mysticism, Buddhism, and depth psychology not only estranged him from orthodox theology but also fostered a commitment to the problem of man's social and natural environment. Along with the insight in the fundamental unity of man and nature goes a concern for the dignity and integrity of natural life in every form. The language of St. Francis of Assisi addressing sun, birds, and flowers is no longer possible in poetry, of course, but there is an affinity of emotional tone behind Sjöstrand's more sophisticated diction. An example is his praise of the mollusc, Littorina littorea:

> o snails!
> Ordinary everyday snails
> for bait and tossing games!
>
> You,
> the most ordinary of them all—
> what names we've thoughtlessly
> heaped on you:
> unpoetic,
> thickheaded,
> spineless,
> mollusc!
>
> I saw you
> and I call you by name:
> *Littorina littorea!*
>
> I recognize myself
> in you who have gills
> and free-swimming larvae[28]

We can thus discern an inner logic in Sjöstrand's development during the 1960's: liberated from catholic, rationalistic doctrine, he was thrown back upon his own inner resources, and a renewed abandonment to the uncertain waters of the unconscious brought about a new understanding of the modern scientific approach to the world and a realization, before it had become current fashion, that man must stop his naive and cruel exploitation of nature and awaken to his responsibility for the future of earth as the home of life. Of course this development was no logically ordered process, nor were these ideas and concerns entirely new to him. But it is essential to emphasize the unity of vision behind the different aspects of his poetry treated separately in Chapters 3 and 4.

The first book of poetry to be wholly dominated by this new constellation of ideas was *In the Sign of Aquarius* (1967), one of Sjöstrand's most important books, deploying his new insights in fields seemingly as different as music, physics, biology, and the philosophy of history, yet containing this diversity in a unified poetic diction.

The year after the *Aquarius* book Sjöstrand took two decisive steps. He formally left the Roman Catholic Church and he left Stockholm. He had remained comparatively isolated in the capital during all the fourteen years since 1954 and had few intimate friends to miss, and contacts with publishers and editors were sufficiently well established not to require his presence on the spot. What drove him away was a growing disgust with the sterility and conformity of metropolitan life, a need for natural surroundings to support his inner life. So he and his wife eagerly accepted an offer from two patrons of the arts, the distinguished couple Alva and Gunnar Myrdal, to move into an old and picturesque house in the small town of Mariefred on Lake Mälaren, about one hour's railway journey from Stockholm. Mariefred is a town of medieval origin, beautifully situated on the waterfront, boasting a sixteenth-century castle and small enough to give its residents almost the feeling of living in the country. Though quite different from his native coastal landscape, the new surroundings brought Sjöstrand into renewed contact with his own element: his drawing-room windows look onto the lake, and in the small harbor lies his own boat. Moving to Mariefred meant reestablishing the literal meaning of his name.[29] It was a kind of return home, but spiritually it was a new departure.

The first years in Mariefred brought anything but relaxation and peace, however. Though deeply satisfied with his new environment, his mind was not at peace. To the strain of removal and acclimatization were added passing but pointed financial difficulties which led to overwork. In 1971 he brought out no less than four books: a collection of essays, *The Necessity of*

Imagination; two books of translations, of the Greek poet Yannis Ritsos and the French poet Yves Bonnefoy; and a collection of his own poetry, *The Dream is No Façade*. Some of the pieces in this latter book are in the character of transcriptions of dreams, voices, and visions, and the symptoms of psychic disturbance are manifest, even emphasized. The publication of it testifies to an important trait in the personality of the author, his moral courage.

V *The Price of Creativity*

Mention of conflicts, crises, and psychic disturbances has been the burden of this biographical sketch, and the matter calls for special discussion in order to avoid misunderstanding and to explain Sjöstrand's views on the problem of creativity and on the artist's position in society.

Psychiatric diagnoses are notoriously precarious and the concept of mental illness, in itself ambiguous, must be used with special care in connection with creative artists. Creativity as such may be said to constitute an abnormal mode of behavior, and artists and poets have been known to court madness and cultivate mental derangement in order to enhance their creative powers; Rimbaud is one instance that comes to mind. On the other hand, art may also be looked upon as an outlet for conflicts which, if barred from expression, could mean a dangerous threat to the personality. These general conditions have a particular relevance to Sjöstrand's psychology of crisis, which is typical in its ambiguity.

The opposite poles of Sjöstrand's mental life during times of crisis are depression and agitated states of mind not seldom accompanied by visions and voices demanding poetic expression. An outspoken example is the poem "Conversation" in the 1971 collection, a conversation "while the lava is still moving," and with a motto from Robert Lowell's "The Fat Man in the Mirror": *"Nurse, it is a person. It is nerves."*

A glance in the mirror
is enough to see that the Balance is disturbed.

Credit and debit? Just look, how the ganglions glow and ache
in the chronic body. We snivel and swell,

or scream, abandoned;
>some throw their children
in the Giant's mouth, flee into want. We rise slowly
towards ourselves! Flutter, prattle.

But the Oppressor continues:
>"I adore no Adam!
(I shall sneak up on you
like a snake, like a dog, like a cat, or
in a human shape no one can tell
from the mortal beings
>>who are and who were!)
. . . .
I look, and I listen.

And the words stumble over the words
as before.

Nozinan or librium.

A fallen sun is glowing in the billow.
>And for sure:
two ducks have drowned
with too much water in their wings.

>✿ ✿ ✿

When the fire is quenched the lava is dumb.[30]

The exact identity of the Oppressor is neither clear nor important
but it is obvious that the lava refers to a kind of burning magma
from the inner life which has broken through the crust of the
socially adapted personality. It is also obvious that this volcanic
eruption is sufficiently disturbing to the poet and his surroundings to call for medical treatment by means of sedatives and
tranquilizers such as nozinan and librium.

The juxtaposition of fire and water in "Conversation" is significant. There is the "sun glowing in the billow" and the drowned
ducks and the fire of the burning lava. Both elements belong,
in Sjöstrand's poetic world, to the interior of the earth which is
also the unconscious soul, and both have a double aspect, one
positive, the other negative. Fire is a destructive but also a purify-

ing element, and life-giving water may also threaten with drowning. In moments of crisis the threat and danger can be overwhelming—a duck drowning in water is a notion real enough but appearing as absurd as a poet being engulfed by his own inspiration, but that is a very real danger to Sjöstrand. The crust of earth containing the liquid, fiery magma and the terra firma opposing the waters of the rivers and oceans are, in consequence, symbols of the conscious, thinking, and ordering mind. This kind of symbolism is of course more or less universal, and since Virgil and Dante the descent into the nether world as image of the descent into the depths of the soul belongs to the central literary tradition. And Æneas has to negotiate not only rivers of water but also the fiery Phlegethon running "flammis torrentibus" (VI, 550).

Now, any descent into any hell is undertaken at the peril of life, and he who makes the venture stands in need of some kind of golden bough. Æneas was aided in his search for the bough by his mother Venus, goddess of love, and the divine female figure of Wisdom in many of Sjöstrand's poems seems to have a similar function.[31] Dante's substitution of a magic formula for Virgil's golden bough is of course well known to Sjöstrand: the Charon of Dante's *Inferno* is placated by the words

> vuolsi cosí colà, dove si puote
> ciò che si vuole (III: 95 f.)

> (It is so willed where will and power are one. [Sinclair])

That is to say, the pilgrim is to be allowed passage over the river because it is God's will. Correspondingly, Sjöstrand would regard the artist's descent into himself as a mission undertaken under the auspices of love and a divine purpose, and the sufferings of the creative artist as a kind of vicarious suffering yielding insights that can benefit his fellowmen. But it is a gamble with high stakes:

> Since the dreams have abandoned him: the mental hospital or the cross? No home-town, or birthplace, where he can recognize himself—[32]

Abandoning the metaphors of mythology and theology and returning to the psychological aspects of Sjöstrand's sufferings, it would seem that his was a case singularly suited for psychoanalytical treatment according to the Freudian school. His "neurosis" would probably have been explained as a result of the emotional deprivation of his early youth—a hypothesis that could be corroborated by the fact that those who shared the same emotional environment, his sister and brother, both developed similar symptoms. And the conjunction of adolescent crises with a general sense of guilt would surely lend itself to interpretations along the lines of Freud's theories of sexuality. But Sjöstrand seems deliberately to have avoided exposing himself to psychoanalytical treatment, although Freud was topical enough in the Gothenburg circles where Sjöstrand moved in the late forties. One reason was that he had witnessed disastrous results of such treatment—the suicide of an authoress of that circle was commonly attributed to a course of analysis that got out of hand. There was also the fear voiced by many poets before him that a successful "cure" might dry up the springs of creativity.

Instead of the positivistic, deterministic approach of Freudian psychology Sjöstrand chose to interpret his situation in terms of Existentialist philosophy and Thomist theology, both of which stress man's free will and are hence liable to strengthen rather than mitigate the sense of guilt and moral responsibility. For Sjöstrand the Christian doctrine of atonement seems to have remained merely a doctrine with no operative force in his personal case.

It was in this predicament that Jungian psychology seemed to offer new opportunities. Not, like Freud, denying the validity of religious experience, Jung looks for common psychological patterns in all religions, and in linking the dreams, visions, and obsessions of his patients not only with their personal pasts, as did Freud, but with a common heritage of experience clothed in a common language of symbols, he encouraged creativity instead of denigrating it as a symptom of illness.

Both Freudians and Jungians emphasize the equilibrium of the conscious and the unconscious as the sign of a healthy, normal human being. The control of reason over primitive fears and urges would be the narrow positivistic way of putting it; the mutual interpenetration of mind and soul, of spirit and nature, would be the mystic or Romantic formula. Naturally Sjöstrand inclined toward the latter, but not even in his most excessive abandonment to mystical and Jungian modes of thought does his skeptic rationalism forsake him. When his symptoms of mental illness appear he clearly recognizes them for what they are and seeks proper treatment at the hands of such psychiatrists as he feels he can trust to be responsible human beings and expert dispensers of drugs. But at the same time he asserts the human and artistic validity of the very experiences of which he wishes to be cured. The contradiction involved in this attitude is only superficial. He seeks help to survive as a man fit to live and work, which implies pacifying the eruptive forces by artificial means, but that does not exclude him from acknowledging the value and meaning of these eruptions and putting them to poetic use. Much is to be gained "while the lava is still moving."

Not all of Sjöstrand's poetry is conceived in such dramatic fashion, of course. The deeper creative layers of the personality may become manifest in more peaceful ways, too, as for instance in dreams. "Dream" is a recurrent word in his work and seems, psychologically, to cover anything from normal dreams to the most startling hallucinations. Epistemologically, he sees dreams as a source of knowledge: as a means of communication with the collective unconscious Jung speaks of, or with "unconscious nature," to use the language of the Romantics that Sjöstrand first studied under the guidance of Béguin's book on Dreams and the Romantic Spirit.[33]

It is this comprehensive meaning of the word that Sjöstrand refers to in the title, *The Dream is No Façade*, and whenever that phrase appears in the book. For example, in "Counter-Images":

> Like antiworlds.
> Like near-invisible antibodies
> (forcing contagion
> and disease back)
> are the rapporteurs of the deep dream.
> . . . .
> The dream is no façade.[34]

The phrase also appears in the very first poem of the book, there with an explanatory addition:

> I thought: poetry—the stretching of the inner bedrock:
> each man set before his own choice,
> not the peoples.
>
> The dream is no façade.
> Poetry no flight from the world that is!
> and could be.[35]

Which means that he who creates out of his innermost self is no poetic escapist shirking his responsibilities toward society. For it is deep down at the bottom of the soul that all men are alike; there lies the foundation of universal equality and brotherhood.

The whole of Sjöstrand's work is built on the conviction, or hope, that the dreams and visions of his own self have their counterparts in images hidden inside everybody, and that his poetry may help to free and elevate those images into the light of consciousness and thus give them meaning. In this view, a poem is not a message from author to reader or listener, but rather a key for decoding the symbolic messages everyone receives in inarticulate emotional modes of experience such as dreaming or meditating or listening to music.

To return to the lava metaphor, we can say that in the experiences where the inner life forces itself into everyday consciousness, producing the raw substance of poetry, materials of utterly different origins have been fused in the process. Personal memories from early childhood fuse with recent, often trivial impressions from the immediate surroundings, headlines, and catchwords from newspapers and conversations with profound ideas and images from sustained studies, rhythms of everyday life with refined musical patterns. In this Sjöstrand is surely not different from other poets, but perhaps he differs with regard to the scope of the material integrated in his poetry. The scientific influences on his work, for instance, are not a matter of mere allusions to current ideas. He suffers his personal experience of the world to be structured by these ideas. And the full range of meaning of the word "suffer" is relevant here. Accommodating his emotional experience to, say, the relativity of the physicists' models of the universe is not an intellectual game only; it is a process of fusing different materials at high pressure and intense emotional temperatures, and such processes always involve dangers to the vessel. It is a matter of the Symbolists' "alchemie du verbe" come true in a more literal way than was ever imagined by the inventor of that formula. Alchemists and nuclear physicists both know that they perform their experiments at their own peril.

Sjöstrand has also given much thought to the theoretical problems of creativity. Among his comprehensive reading on the subject one book deserves special mention, Arthur Koestler's *The Act of Creation* (1964). One of the theses of Koestler's book is that, psychologically and intellectually, the act of creation is essentially the same whether it is classified under scientific discovery, mystic insight, or artistic production. Speaking of one of the allegorical types he employs to clarify his line of thought Koestler sums up:

This last figure, the White Magician, symbolizes the *self-transcending element* in the scientist's motivational drive and emotional make-up; his humble immersion into the mysteries of nature, his quest for the harmony of the spheres, the origins of life, the equations of a unified field theory. The conquistadorial urge is derived from a sense of power, the participatory urge from a sense of oceanic wonder. "Men were first led to the study of natural philosophy," wrote Aristotle, "as indeed they are today, by wonder." Maxwell's earliest memory was "lying on the grass, looking at the sun, and *wondering*." Einstein struck the same chord when he wrote that whoever is devoid of the capacity to wonder, "whoever remains unmoved, whoever cannot contemplate or know the deep shudder of the soul in enchantment, might just as well be dead for he has already closed his eyes upon life."
This oceanic feeling of wonder is the common source of religious mysticism, of pure science and art for art's sake; it is their common denominator and emotional bond.[36]

With this Sjöstrand wholeheartedly agrees, and it would be wrong not to emphasize the positive, happy feelings involved in the writing of his poetry. What Koestler fails to point out in this context, however, is that self-transcendence is not only a

consummation devoutly to be wished by all men obsessed with
the creative urge, but constitutes a mortal threat of annihilation
to the self of everyday life and common sense. Some mystics
and saints seem to have been endowed with the fortunate ability
to walk in and out of their transcendent worlds without suffering
any anguish of passage, without being affected in the least in the
capacity to fulfill their worldly tasks. Others, however, perhaps
the majority of creative men and women, have jeopardized their
mental equilibrium in the pursuit of their art. Sjöstrand is certainly one for whom the wonder and the pain, the grace and
the damnation, of creative life are inseparable. But the damnation
of one may serve the salvation of another:

"I am a pharmacist—I transform poisons into remedies. . . . And moreover I am here to seek the Father, or the Abyss; the Incomprehensible,
which is also Silence . . ."[37]

CHAPTER 2

Poetry and Music

I *Musical Background*

EVERY self-respecting poet within the Symbolist tradition felt obliged to pay his tribute to music as the paragon of the arts, and if Östen Sjöstrand were only another one of all these composers in *blanc majeur* and experimenters in poetic sonata form, he could be dismissed as of no particular consequence in the field of musical poetry. There are earlier and more startling examples of such formal experimentation in Swedish literature, *e.g.* in the works of Gunnar Ekelöf and Erik Lindegren, and of course the precedents set by the French Symbolists, by Valéry and by Eliot, were to be followed by many other poets. Now, all these have taught Sjöstrand important lessons in the art of applying musical forms of composition to poetry, and he has pointed out both Eliot and Valéry as decisive influences. But in his knowledge of music he excels these masters and, more important, his experiments involve a much more sophisticated type of musical diction. None of the other poets mentioned have ventured further than, say, Stravinsky in their musical taste and understanding, but Sjöstrand, being much younger, has worked in close contact with the avant-garde music of the 1950's and 1960's and has even provided words for electrophonic compositions. Studying his work, we have to reconsider many of our assumptions about the ways in which music and literature can influence each other, and irrespective of his artistic achievements in this field, his attempts to keep pace with the most recent tendencies in music have the general interest we find in any pioneering work.

Sjöstrand set out from a wholly traditional musical background, and his first musico-poetic exercises in the late 1940's were related to Debussy. The family concerts at the home of the

Sjöstrands have already been mentioned. His father's playing the violin or the piano and his mother's singing formed part of his immediate surroundings as a small boy and made classical music and simple folk music a natural element of life, as obviously enjoyable as swimming, or reading storybooks, or playing with animals. It is worth stressing the connection in Sjöstrand's experience between such innocent pastimes of childhood and the classical music of the eighteenth and nineteenth centuries. The collapse of his childhood world following upon his father's death was, he says, like an expulsion from a garden of Eden.[1] After came the years of adolescent suffering and insecurity, and whatever belonged to the world before the "fall" formed part of a happy whole, a simple paradise to which he could look back nostalgically but which he could never hope to regain. The music associated with this paradise was above all the chamber music of Vienna classicism and nineteenth-century Romanticism—Beethoven, Schubert, Brahms. This was often music of an uncomplicated kind, immediately intelligible to ear and soul. Not a few of the piano trios of these composers, which were frequently performed at his home, express a simple joy of making music together, a characteristic which seems lost to much contemporary music.

If classical music belonged to childhood, Sjöstrand's adolescent years in the *gymnasium* were in part devoted to jazz and dance music, a natural reaction to an austere upbringing and, besides, the fashion among higher-form schoolboys in Sweden at that time. Occasionally, Sjöstrand can still let himself go at the piano, but only as a reminiscent joke. He also blew the trumpet, "full of defiance and opposition."[2] Otherwise, he has not developed his talents as a performer, but devoted himself to comprehensive reading of and about music and to active listening, often with the score at hand. During his Stockholm years he had ample opportunities to attend opera and concerts, and he is also a great listener to broadcast and recorded music; a hi-fi set is a prominent feature of his living room.

Sjöstrand's musical learning is wide and he is thoroughly familiar with the common repertoire of concert halls and opera houses. But apart from his special interest in Debussy, he shares the taste of most of his professional friends, *i.e.* a tendency to disregard the period from, say, the death of Johann Sebastian Bach to the appearance of Igor Stravinsky. Important exceptions should be noted, however. Mozart, for instance, is a composer he often refers to, both as the supreme master, in the operas, of musical psychology, and as an esoteric mystic and philosopher of death in his last works, especially *The Magic Flute* and the *Requiem.* "In some mysterious way," he once wrote, "music always seems to be turned towards death."[3]

Naturally enough, his musical predilections often have a literary coloring. The masonic symbolism of *The Magic Flute* is not purely musical, and in the case of Alexander Scriabin, to whom Sjöstrand has devoted an essay called "The Poem of Fire and Ecstasy,"[4] the religious, metaphysical ideas he strove to embody in his later compositions, particularly in the *Prometheus* symphony, can hardly be grasped without the aid of words. In fact, the interrelations of music and literature and the mutual enrichment of the two are among Sjöstrand's chief concerns as a writer of poetry and of opera libretti.

One can distinguish two opposite poles in his relationship to music and in his musical taste. One is the passionately romantic, metaphysical profundity represented by Scriabin, and the other is the typically Gallic *esprit* and intellectualism of the art of composers such as Ravel. It is no coincidence that the essay on Scriabin in his book *The Necessity of Imagination* is followed by one entitled "Maurice Ravel—an Ironist?" Correspondingly, there are two sides to the impact of music on Sjöstrand's poetry. One is a matter of tone and feeling, of the deepest emotional content of his art; the other of structure and form.

The methodological problems involved in the comparison between music and literature are not to be treated lightly, as appears from the comprehensive critical literature on the subject.[5] However, it seems unnnecessary to consider these problems in principle here, for they will be raised in the course of the following analyses and commentaries. And whatever the general legitimacy of interpreting poetry in musical terms, Sjöstrand himself insists upon such an interpretation of his own works.

II *The Discovery of Debussy*

Sjöstrand's awakening to the expressive possibilities of music occurred at the same time as he first groped his way toward the expressive possibilities of words, or, rather, his discovery of music helped him to find that way. And it was one composer in particular who came to act as the releaser of his pent-up emotions, Claude Debussy, and among Debussy's compositions above all the *Préludes* and other pieces for the piano. It is impossible to give an objective psychological account of what happened in Sjöstrand's mind when Debussy's art set his emotional experience free and transformed it into verse. That such things do happen is beyond doubt, but the science of the mind is not yet sufficiently advanced to tell us how they happen. That remains part of the enigma of artistic creativity. This is Sjöstrand's own account of his poetic awakening:

Although I was not altogether a stranger to the power of words, poetry came to me like a revelation, a sudden eruption. And the catalysts—in the solitude of the final choice—were Paul Valéry and Claude Debussy. . . . It was music that opened the floodgates and gave free course to the waters. With Valéry, the origin of a poem often was an inner, impelling rhythm. My head was full of rhythmic figures: everything I heard around me—from the spoon in the teacup to the movement·of tram wheels and elevators—I immediately associated, reflexively, with this music by Claude Debussy which occupied me completely. I made Debussy's rhythmic figures my starting point, searched for words to them: the rhythmic patterns objectified my dreams, the images from my inner life. (Music became my equivalent of the spots on Da Vinci's wall—this enigma of perception which no psychologist can ever explain satisfactorily.)[6]

What can be done, however, in default of psychological explanations, is to compare the particular music that acted as stimulant with the poetry that finally ensued, in order to ascertain similarities of content or structure.

But first we must go one step backwards, behind the music itself. At the very time when Sjöstrand was struggling with his first poetic attempts there appeared a book in Swedish, *Claude Debussy*, by Kajsa Rootzén, which naturally attracted his attention. In it the author quotes some significant words of the composer himself concerning the deepest sources of his work: "Who knows the secret of musical creation? The roar of the sea, the curvature of a horizontal line, the rustle of leaves in the wind, the crying of a bird; they all leave a variety of impressions in our minds. And suddenly, without any conscious effort, one of these memories wells forth from the depths of the soul and seeks an outlet in music. It has a harmony of its own, and any attempt to find a truer and better one is in vain."[7]

The relevance of these words to Sjöstrand is twofold. First, many of his poems have been created from the same psychic materials as Debussy's works, from impressions of natural elements and sceneries, stored and transformed in the unconscious mind: the sea, the horizon, the wind, leaves, birds—they all form recurrent motifs in his poetry as in Debussy's music. Second, music created from such materials seems to have had the effect of reviving his unconscious memories of such sensuous impressions and helping him to articulate them in words. Sjöstrand may be said to express, in many of his early poems, in words what Debussy expressed in music, and to do it with that music as a releasing stimulant.

So far, the parallel between the two has been stated in rather abstract terms. It is easy to give it more substance, however, since Debussy has indicated the "content" of several of his compositions by means of more or less fanciful titles. Many of these titles refer to water and wind, which are also the dominant elements in Sjöstrand's poetic imagery. One of Debussy's most famous orchestral compositions is, of course, called *La mer*, and among his piano pieces we find "Reflets dans l'eau" (*Images*, I), "Le vent dans la plaine," "Ce qu'a vu le vent d'ouest" (*Préludes*, I) and others with reference to the same elements. And the windy, watery character of Debussy's music is not restricted to the titles he chose for his compositions. The new harmonies he employed, the new pedal technique, and other strictly musical features of his work lend to it a flowing, dripping, breezy, glittering, billowing, stormy character, as the case may be.

But Debussy is no mere impressionist in the sense that his sole aim is to reproduce the natural sounds experienced by the ear.

Kajsa Rootzén emphasizes this in her book: "We must always remember that Amiel's famous words about the landscape as a state of mind very much apply to Claude Debussy. What he 'paints' in his 'Reflets dans l'eau' is not only the trembling reflexions, the glittering light, the quiet movement of the waves upon the face of the water, it is also a mood, an inner experience."[8] Perhaps it is wise not to proceed further in the metaphorical interpretation of Debussy's water symbolism and inquire into its psychological meaning; such interpretations are more legitimate applied to verbal works of art.[9]

In spite of their impressionism, many of Debussy's works for the piano have structures modeled upon elaborate traditional forms of composition; "Reflets dans l'eau," for instance, is a full-fledged *ricercare*. Sjöstrand's early poetry, however, rarely adopts any complicated formal arrangements of words and imagery. The musical effect he creates is more like striking a few chords on the keyboard.

In his second book of poems, Sjöstrand has evolved a limited but well-rounded form adaptable both to impressionistic miniatures and epigrammatic statements of ideas and beliefs: it is a simple pentastich with a break between the first three, often slightly longer lines and the concluding couplet. An example illustrating the application of this form to the wind-water theme:

> Water caves, wind cells,
> spaces for want and impotence,
> . homes for imagined fish and unseen wings.
>
> O stratowave of thought
> at sighting and scenting.[10]

This little poem clearly demonstrates the double function of the elemental imagery to be found also in Debussy's music: on the one hand the sensuousness and rhythm of the imagery which bring the bodily experiences of weight and lightness, of sight and smell to resound; and on the other, the inner symbolism implied. The caves and cells are obviously located in the soul since they are occupied by want and impotence and are the home of the dreamt-of fish and unseen wings, *i.e.* hidden, unconscious capacities for navigating the inner waters and using the wings of the spirit. As we shall see, water and wind in Sjöstrand's work generally stand for unconscious soul and spirit, respectively.

One particular piano piece of Debussy haunts many of Sjöstrand's poems, the tenth in the first book of *Préludes*, with the title "La Cathédrale engloutie," "The Engulfed Cathedral." It is one of the best known and at the same time most mysterious of Debussy's works, and has attracted a considerable body of commentary. A useful analysis is provided by Debussy's friend, E. Robert Schmitz, in his *The Piano Works of Claude Debussy*, which Sjöstrand remembers having read. Schmitz speaks of "the opening 'gutted' chords, organum in parallel fourths and octaves [which] seem to evoke in Debussy structures of the past, not presently visible."[11] These chords illustrate, within the epic framework of the composition, the calm sea out of which the cathedral is to rise at dawn, but their emotional tone is ambivalent in its hollowness. Of the composer's use of this kind of "gutted" chords Schmitz also writes, "Besides the clarity of color it offers through the omission of the acoustically out-of-tune, and opaque third of the triad, it also has the advantage of leaving the modality (whether major or minor) undetermined for the moment, opening two horizons to the listener's ear."[12]

As we shall see, Sjöstrand made use of the legend behind "The Engulfed Cathedral," but he also created verbal parallels to the harmonic effect of the characteristic chords just described. Without being too fanciful, I think the following poem from *Unio* might be interpreted in that way:

> in the swirling
> in the bright depths of water
> I saw the earth's broken certainty annulled
> by the water columns of dusk
>
> in the swirling
> in the bright depths of water
> I saw the dawn's sail
> bulge with life
> I saw the wind
> I saw the wind

hush in space
I saw the stars
the pale ones
become leaves
become forests of greenery

in the swirling
in the watery depths of light
I saw the manifest made manifest
I saw[13]

With all its visual imagery, this poem remains "undetermined,"
to use Schmitz's word; deliberately undetermined as to the
precise content of the poet's vision, even as to the emotional
tone: the water columns of dusk glide into the sails of dawn.
It is undetermined as the elements of wind and water themselves,
capable of innumerable metamorphoses. The hollow or "gutted"
sonority is further enhanced by the use of abstract words with no
specific reference, such as "broken certainty" and "the manifest
made manifest."

The only touch of color in the poem, analogous to a change
to more colorful sonority in the harmonies of Debussy's music,
is provided by the greenness of the foliage of the woods. This
progression from colorlessness to color, which is neither a modula-
tion nor a development, seems to have interested Sjöstrand as a
technical problem in verse; he returns to it a few years later
in the opening stanza of a longer poem.[14]

In general, when writers claim to have used musical forms in
literary compositions, we may be wise to respond with caution.
Even when a verbal description of a musical structure seems to
fit a poem exactly, it must not be forgotten that it is the verbal
description that fits, not the music as such. This qualification
applies to any comparison between the arts and should always
be borne in mind, but in the case of Debussy's influence on
Sjöstrand there are not only the similarities of musical and poetic
forms of expression but a certain amount of verbal material
attached to the music as well as verbal commentaries to the compositions known to the poet. Rootzén's book was published the
year before Sjöstrand's first collection of poetry appeared,

Schmitz's the same year as his second collection, and he has read them both. The literary quality of "The Engulfed Cathedral" is obvious. It is, in one of its aspects, a piece of program music built on an old Celtic legend according to which the city of Ys, situated on the western coast of Brittany, was engulfed by the ocean some time in the fourth or fifth century A.D. It was protected against the sea by a dike, and in that dike was a secret floodgate. The king himself guarded the key to the gate, but one night, after a wild banquet, his daughter stole the key and opened the gates and let the waters of the ocean submerge the city. At dawn when the sea is calm, the cathedral can still be seen rising out of the depths and its bells can be heard chiming. This legend was turned into an opera by the French composer Edouard Lalo and was performed with great success in Paris in 1888, the year after Debussy's return to Paris from his long sojourn in Rome. Now, his *Prélude*, written some twenty years later, does not recount the story, it only illustrates its epilogue so to speak, the emergence of the cathedral from the calm sea and its return into the depths.[15]

The legend shows obvious parallels to the story of the sub-merged Atlantis, and combines the age-old myth of divine punishment by water with the Christian Catholic conception of the restoring powers of the Church. And, according to Schmitz, "In Debussy a third element must be added, his pagan rite of the sea, equally esoteric, equally strong."[16] In Sjöstrand's poetry the legend is a recurrent theme, associated with Ys or Atlantis or both, and with the same combination of mythical, Christian, and pagan elements. In *Unio* he writes of "my cities submerged by the sea," in *Consecration* he alludes to Atlantis twice, in *A Winter in the North* he refers to "cities and stone submerged," and in *The Sign of Aquarius* he explicitly mentions "the sunk cathedral's bells."[17]

In its fullest development this theme appears in *Poems between Midnight and Dawn*, published in 1954 when Debussy was still an important source of inspiration. If we look at the third of the seven poems in the set, we can see, in its middle two stanzas, a contrast which clearly illustrates Sjöstrand's spiritual situation at that time:

Concealed world with gates closed fast
where night wells in with its huge wave
    annihilating the piled bulwarks of the years;
stars encircle the columns of the deeps
and drowned bells swing in the purifying phosphorescence.

Revealed world that calms my disbelief
that opens a heaven in Gothic woods;
    the stems grow out from the heart of innocence:
look, the sundial angel listens to the song of the universe,
and those who adore Your speechless light, and petrify.[18]

The hidden world of the first stanza is obviously the submerged
Ys with its cathedral, which on the symbolical level of interpretation stands for the hidden, inner world of man submerged in the
dark waters of the subconscious soul. Against this submarine
world is set the picture of another cathedral, perhaps Chartres,
lifting its columns toward the sky, bathed in air and sunshine.
The two stanzas and the two cathedrals stand against each other
as darkness against light, water against air, soul against spirit,
a world of opaque symbols against one of transfigured reality, of
hidden poetic intuition against revealed religious truth. If the
musico-poetic impulse is primary in Sjöstrand's creative work
and the interpretation in Christian and other terms secondary,
the submerged cathedral is the primary symbol and forms part
of his immediate inner experience of the fall, the loss of innocent
glory and holiness. In consequence, the antithesis between the
two stanzas is not a static dichotomy but phases of a development. When, after his conversion, he entered the cathedrals of
Catholic Christendom, whether they were built in Gothic
architecture or Thomist theology, he believed that here his
submarine world of desires and emotional conflicts was lifted
up out of the depths and transfigured. The *Poems between Midnight and Dawn* form the strongest expression of this particular
belief in all Sjöstrand's work.

Returning to Debussy's composition, we find the same dual
aspect of the cathedral. What Rootzén refers to as the inner
landscape and Schmitz as "the pagan rite of the sea" corresponds
to Sjöstrand's pre-Christian elemental, psychic experience. The

Catholic implications of Debussy's composition may not be quite so evident, but Schmitz is surely not unduly fanciful when, looking at the piano score from some distance, he finds that "few are the measures which do not contribute to graphic representation, of one form of arch or another."[19] Debussy's cathedral is not only built to be heard by the ear, but to be seen by the eye of the player. Moreover, there is a distinct influence on Debussy, in the tenth prelude as elsewhere, of old medieval modes and Gregorian chants which reinforce the religious overtones of the composition. To close the circle of associations, it may be mentioned that Sjöstrand has confessed that he—and he claims to be far from the only one—"always associates the Gregorian chant with the sea wave, the common oceanic motion."[20] So water, music, poetry, and religion are all integrated into one common field of experience and expression.

The parallels between Debussy and Sjöstrand must not be drawn out too far, however. Debussy was hardly a believing Christian; his education may have been conventionally Catholic but his creed was of a more pantheistic kind, which of course was no obstacle to his using modes and forms and motifs with distinctly Catholic associations. A quite different side of Debussy's personality, reflected in his music, should also be mentioned: the sybaritic, sensualistic side so dominant in the composer's private life, so evident in the exquisite play with sonorities in his music. It would be utterly wrong to deny such traits in Sjöstrand's personality, but they are held in strong check by his puritanical morality. In fact, that is one of the reasons why Debussy meant so much to him during those early years when he strove desperately to reconcile the demands of the flesh and the spirit. Abandoning himself to Debussy's music, he could indulge his sensual self without scruple, perhaps without quite knowing what he was doing.

On a level far deeper than any intellectual structures or verbal connotations, deeper than the sonority and harmony of the music, lies that element which Sjöstrand singles out in the essay quoted above: the rhythm, the rhythmic patterns as releasing agents. However, since rhythm is something quite different from definable meters and measures, it is impossible to analyze or demonstrate the creative process by which musical rhythms are transformed into images and words. A discussion of the rhythmic origins of poetry easily ends in psychological hypotheses even less verifiable than comparisons between the arts. In order to hint at the wide implications of this subject and to counterbalance any undue stressing of the importance of Debussy and of music in general, it may be well to draw attention to the other decisive influence upon Sjöstrand's early poetry, Paul Valéry.

In his explanation of the different stages in the birth of a poem, Valéry emphasizes the generative powers of rhythm. Speaking of the origins of his well-known poem "Le Cimetière marin," he tells us that it "began within myself by the simple indication of a rhythm which little by little assumed a meaning."[21] This primary preoccupation of the poet with rhythm is not only a parallel to the rhythmic inspiration of a composer of music; according to Valéry it is, in its earliest phase, indistinguishable from musical inspiration. "The person who knows that music is not his mode of expression had not yet asserted himself in me when my rhythm imposed itself upon me, just as the person who knows that he cannot fly has not yet asserted himself in one who dreams that he is flying."[22]

Studying Valéry as he did at the time of his first creative attempts, Sjöstrand thus found the same insistence on the musical, rhythmic foundations of poetic expression as he had discovered for himself when trying to articulate feelings generated by music. A further parallel between Debussy and Valéry, which no doubt struck him as significant, is their preoccupation with the element of water: the sea and the submarine world are, of course, dominant themes in "Le Cimetière marin."

III Operatic Exercises

While immersed in Debussy's waters Sjöstrand began to feel the need of musical impulses of a more intellectually stimulating kind. "I sought theoretical incitements in Hindemith, Stravinsky,"[23] he states with reference to the late 1940's, when he was still living in Gothenburg. He also mentions Gösta Nystroem, a native of Gothenburg who, however, probably had more to say to Sjöstrand as the composer of *Sinfonia del Mare* and other maritime pieces, than as a formal innovator. It was not until after he settled in Stockholm in 1954 that his interest in contemporary music deepened into one of his serious concerns as an artist. As mentioned in the previous chapter, avant-garde music was prospering there under official patronage.

In Stockholm he also found an opera house of international standard where creative contributions were sought not only from composers but also from poets. Up to the early 1950's most operas on the repertoire of the Royal Theater in Stockholm were performed with little regard to the translation of the libretti. Everything was, and still is, sung in Swedish, but more often than not the translations were of an appallingly low literary standard. In an effort to redress this shortcoming and thereby also to enhance the general artistic prestige of the opera, renowned poets were commissioned to make new translations. Erik Lindegren, for instance, provided new texts for Mozart's *Don Giovanni* and Verdi's *Un Ballo in Maschera*. The translators were not only required to produce poetically convincing solutions but also to pay attention to the musical aspects of the text, *e.g.* the color and quality of stressed vowels, in order to reinforce the tone of the musical phrase and help the singer attain the right effect. This called for poets with considerable musical education.

This new interest in the opera libretto as a literary genre was not restricted to the traditional repertoire. New works by foreign composers were handed over to competent poets, and their help and collaboration were requested by Swedish composers with operatic projects. Thus Erik Lindegren and Karl-Birger Blomdahl together created two operas, *Aniara* and *Herr von Hancken*. With his passion for music, Sjöstrand was well suited to this kind of work, and he has tried his hand both as a translator and as a writer of original libretti. Among his translations are two Gluck operas *Iphigénie en Aulide* and *Alceste*, the Italian composer Luigi Dallapiccola's *Volo di notte*, commissioned by Swedish television, Stravinsky's *The Rake's Progress*, and Händel's *Messiah*. His original works include the cantata *A Play of Mary, Mother of Jesus* and the two-act opera *The Banquet*, both set to music, in 1958, by Sven-Erik Bäck.

As a translator, Sjöstrand takes greatest pride in his Swedish version of W. H. Auden's and Chester Kallman's text for *The Rake's Progress*, published in 1961. Among the problems involved in this work he mentions "Words and sentences which must follow the motions and changes of the music, its repetitions and contrasts. Certain text groups which must lend themselves to being lifted out of the sentence for the purpose of fugal treatment ... parallel sections where different texts support each other while the quality of the vowels have to coincide (often by rhyming). Well, clearly I want the translation judged not according to the original text but according to the score."[24] The outcome of these labors was highly satisfactory, so much so that Stravinsky himself, on hearing his own opera sung in Swedish without understanding a word of the language, pronounced this text better than the original English text.[25] Besides, Sjöstrand's interest in *The Rake's Progress* was manifest several years before he undertook the translation. The poem "Adonis in Bedlam" in *Return* is a free paraphrase of the concluding scene of the opera.[26]

Adjusting words to a finished score is one thing, creating an opera in close collaboration with the composer is quite a different thing. That is how *The Banquet* came into existence. The plot and characters were of Sjöstrand's invention, but "the music, or the projected course of musical events, came to a very great extent to deliver words and sentences ... which perhaps would never have been uttered except for that music, through which experience from both dreams and waking life were materialized into words."[27] The word "deliver" with its connotation of giving birth is important; as we have seen, Sjöstrand described the effect of Debussy's music on him as a kind of midwifery, in the Socratic sense. And now he again insists on the organic nature of the process. It would be tempting to borrow the terminology of semiotics and communication theory and speak of the music as a "code" by means of which images and words are shaped into a meaningful message; only that this does not explain what really happens any more than the organic metaphors. In his attempts to convey the nature of this mystery of poetic creativity, Sjöstrand also resorts to metaphors derived from inorganic chemistry: he compares the musical structures absorbed by the poet's mind to axes of verbal crystallization.[28]

The effect may have been the same in the case of *The Banquet*, but Bäck's music is certainly very different from Debussy's, as could be expected of a composer so much younger—Bäck was born in 1919. It is difficult to give an idea in words of the general qualities of the variegated score of *The Banquet*, which is full of stylistic parody and reminiscences. Unfortunately the score has not been published.[29]

The text of one passage from the first act of the opera, which is repeated in the second act, has been published as a separate poem. Sjöstrand has commented upon it himself: "It is a madrigal spontaneously prompted by a musical structure of which I had a rough idea before it was definitely formulated [by the composer]. Now it so happened that after the opera was finished, this madrigal continued to grow within me, new lines appeared; there was something further which demanded expression. And the musical pattern that determined the shaping of the poem continued to grow, too."[30]

> Night came, and sickness struck me with silence,
> paralysed my eye and my foot,
> it paralysed my eye and my foot.
>
> The Physician came, and the Physician said to me:
> for this night there is no cure,
> there is no cure.
>
> Love came, and love said to me:
> the night may hide your being, your root
> but it cannot hide—that spark
>
> that spark that dwells in your innermost space
> —and burns, beyond the reach of night.

The Lord is the protagonist of the opera, he is the ruler of an Italian state during the Renaissance but he is also the ruler of a number of citizens within himself, not all of them as obedient and subservient as could be wished. He is an illustration of the conception of man propounded by depth psychologists, above all C. G. Jung, and Jungian too is Sjöstrand's idea, in the opera, of the total integration of the personality, the individuation, as the ultimate end of spiritual development. It would narrow the scope of the character of this Lord too much to diagnose his malady in any definite terms. It is any depression of the soul—including the poet's own—which threatens to disintegrate the personality and its powers of perception and creativity. It is a malady to be relieved but not cured by medical, psychiatric treatment, as Sjöstrand well knows from his own experience. The only hope lies in the power of Love, here identified with the undying ethereal element of Neo-Platonists and Stoics, or with Meister Eckehart's *scintilla*, at other times in Sjöstrand's work with Poetry, Art, or Wisdom, always an unknown female agent, a true Sophia. Sjöstrand is certainly no dramatist, the essence of the libretto of *The Banquet* is lyrical and lies in its poetry of ideas and emotions.

The enthusiastic hopes for a rejuvenation of the art of the opera that stimulated the work on *The Banquet* were a passing phase. In a dialogue between Sjöstrand and Bäck published in 1966, Sjöstrand speaks of recent opera plans of his left unfinished and he confesses that he fails to see any example of an important innovation in the field of the opera and that "although a lot has been done, and although we [Bäck and himself] have done a great deal ourselves, I have become increasingly doubtful of the concessions one is forced to make with regard to both text and music... After all, opera is too much an art of concessions these days, I believe."[31] Some years earlier, at the time of the completion of *The Banquet*, he had characterized the relationship between music and literature as a "creative tension" from which both arts could benefit,[32] but during the following years he fell back on the one-way traffic established at the beginning of his career, with music as stimulator and releaser and the words released integrated in a poetic work of art independent of the music.

An instance of Sven-Erik Bäck's music drawing forth a poem from Sjöstrand without any reciprocity or collaboration is "Favola," or "Fable," published in 1963 in *A Winter in the*

North. Sjöstrand knew something of Bäck's composition *Favola*
before he heard it for the first time on the radio and immediately
set to work on his poem. He knew that in this work for one
clarinet and percussion, the solo instrument plays the role of
storyteller with the percussion as audience or chorus, as it were,
listening to and commenting upon the "fable" told by the clarinet.
He probably also knew that the emotional tone of the piece was
colored by the recent death of a close friend of the composer's.
Finally, he was familiar with the critical attitude to music hinted
at in the title and much discussed in Bäck's and Sjöstrand's circles
at the time, according to which a piece of music—as well as
any work of art—is not limited in its content to what the composer
thought or intended while writing it; the listener is free to create
his own fiction or "favola" around it. The storyteller and the
burial are motifs in the poem which Sjöstrand took over straight
from Bäck, partly also the concern with the autonomy of the
story, *i.e.* the work of art. And the musical starting point is
clearly to be seen in the poem in the following questions from its
middle section; questions which of course go far beyond the
acoustic phenomena that prompted them:

What does the ringing of bells hide
which reaches us down from the plain: another Sunday,
or the awaited burial
of the lightning's innumerable victims?
What does the insignificant, smallest bell hide
which, hidden in the mountains, yet penetrates the haze
thrusts into the bones of everyone
with its urgent message?
Say, what does it all mean? The whip's unexpected
crack (in the middle of training),
the trembling machine, the drum roll in the middle of
the square, the running steps,
(in the cellar, in the attic)? And the rumble from the
yet untrod upland?[33]

IV *Ligeti and "Burning Alphabet"*

One of the most remarkable instances of poetic inspiration
caused by the hearing of a particular piece of music is Sjöstrand's

"Burning Alphabet" in the collection of 1967, *In the Sign of Aquarius*. In his essay on music and poetry, Sjöstrand states that this poem, which runs to four printed pages, was written in about 15 or 20 minutes, almost without lifting the pen from the paper, after coming home from a concert including the first performance of the Hungarian-born composer György Ligeti's *Requiem*.[34] Sjöstrand does not seem to have contemplated writing such a poem before going to the concert, it was the impact of the music that released thoughts and feelings accumulated during a long time; ripe, pressing for expression, awaiting the necessary stimulus from without. Ligeti's music not only acted as a psychological trigger, it also influenced the form of the poem very deeply. It may seem impossible that a musical composition of extreme complexity, heard for the very first time, can have any significant structural influence on a long poem tossed off, as it were, in about a quarter of an hour. The explanation is probably that Sjöstrand was much better prepared for listening to the music than he knew or recalled when he wrote the essay commenting on the origins of the poem.

Ligeti, who was born in 1923, received his musical education in Budapest but left Hungary for Germany after the rising of 1956. Since 1960 he has paid repeated visits to Stockholm, teaching composition at the Royal Academy of Music and befriending contemporary Swedish avant-garde composers, among them Sven-Erik Bäck. By the middle of the 1960's he had become a prominent figure in the musical life of Stockholm, especially in the circle called Contemporary Music (which as mentioned also publishes a periodical with the same name). When this circle celebrated its tenth anniversary in the spring of 1965, it was natural that Ligeti should be among the composers contributing new works to the festival concert to be held on Sunday evening, the 14th of March. The first half of this concert consisted of Stravinsky's ballet music *Orpheus* and a new work by Bäck, his cello concerto, and after the interval followed the world première of Ligeti's *Requiem*. And the audience included Sjöstrand who afterwards went straight home to his apartment in Vällingby and wrote his "Burning Alphabet."

He had had no opportunity of hearing the *Requiem* before that

evening, but he had two sources of previous information as to the
structure and details of the work he was going to listen to:
through his friend Bäck who attended the rehearsals and through
the issue of *Contemporary Music* which served as a kind of concert program, giving details of the performers and essays explaining the music to be played. Naturally, Sjöstrand prepared himself
for the occasion by reading the commentary on the *Requiem* included in the issue, written by Harald Kaufmann,[35] and having
heard earlier compositions by Ligeti, he must have had some
idea of what he was going to hear. Nevertheless, the actual effect
of the music was wholly unexpected and struck him like
a revelation.

A brief outline of the *Requiem* seems appropriate at this point.
It takes about half an hour to perform and contains four movements, Introitus, Kyrie, De die judicii sequentia, and Lacrimosa.
Ligeti separates the fourth movement from the rest of the
sequence. It is scored for two soloists, two mixed choruses, and
orchestra, all of them combining to produce a sometimes almost
stunning sound effect, foreign but strangely moving. The Introitus
consists of what Kaufmann calls a "Static plane of sound [. . . in
which] chromatically unfolding sonorities gradually move upwards from low to high register." However, this static plane of
sound is made up of "micro-polyphonic" structures so minute
and so thickly superimposed one upon the other that they cannot
be discerned by the listener's ear. To use a fanciful but perhaps
not altogether irrelevant analogy, it is like regarding a slab of
polished stone: all you see is a solid plane, but you know that it
is made up of the invisible micro-motions of atoms and electrons.
Sjöstrand cites another metaphor saying the same thing: it is like
a forest which is experienced as static although its foliage is
perpetually moving in the wind.[36]

A verbal parallel to a sustained, static plane of sound in music
is of course impossible to achieve, and the second and above
all the third movement of the *Requiem* with their more dramatic
structures are easier to relate to "Burning Alphabet." Sjöstrand
claims to have adopted Ligeti's device of contrasting different
blocks of sound by which he probably means the separate para-
graphs of the poem, contrasted by differences in content and tone.

If Ligeti's *Requiem* is to be treated as a releasing agent comparable in its effect on Sjöstrand to Debussy's music some fifteen years earlier, it must be borne in mind that with Ligeti it was not only the sonorities, rhythms, and so forth that worked upon the poet but a vast body of extra-musical associations as well. The tone and general atmosphere of both the mass and the poem are set by the genre as such. A requiem inevitably entails lament, the remembrance of those who were once living and are now dead, of the mortality of humankind and the transience of human achievements. The dark and sorrowful aspects of the requiem mass are further stressed by Ligeti through his omission of the more hopeful parts traditionally belonging to such a mass, the Sanctus and Agnus Dei for instance. His last movement is the Lacrimosa, of which Kaufmann writes: "The chorus is dumbstruck; only the two soloists and a reduced orchestra have survived the end of the world. Beckett's total emptiness, the remaining void, is made into sound." Listening to Ligeti's mass, one often gets an uncanny feeling of witnessing the realization of ideas set forth in an imaginary piece of music, Adrian Leverkühn's "Lamentation" in Thomas Mann's *Doctor Faustus* (1947), a novel much discussed in avant-garde musical circles in Stockholm.[37]

"The end of the world"—those words by Kaufmann indicate that the composition not only expresses a timeless feeling of sorrow and despair but also a sense of historical despair. Ligeti's *Requiem* stands at the end of a long tradition of church music and Christian culture, transcending and annihilating the musical and spiritual content of this tradition. It is a lament of humanity in its historical dimension, a prophecy of despair for the future of man on earth. At least it seems to have inspired such dark intuitions in Sjöstrand when he first listened to it, and released his vision of man's historical progress through millennia of cultures and barbarity in "Burning Alphabet."

The main theme of the poem is in fact derived from the *Requiem*. "The Book is opened" is the phrase beginning the whole poem, and it is repeated three times later on and complemented by the related theme, "I move forward letter by letter," repeated altogether seven times.[38] The identity of this book becomes clear toward the end of the poem: "The Book is opened. There is written all the good, all the evil in life pursued by men." In the text of the *Requiem*:

> Liber scriptus proferetur,
> In quo totum continetur,
> Unde mundus judicetur.

It is the Book of Life in the Revelation of St. John that becomes, in Sjöstrand's poem, the book of the history of man, from the old Chinese civilization through Greek and Roman antiquity up to the present time; a history marked by cruelty and suffering, in which mighty dynasties and proud cultures are but episodes on the way toward the final Judgment. Thus the poem is very simple in its general outline: the metaphor of the book in which the poet moves forward from letter to letter forms its backbone and corresponds to the history of mankind which is indicated by a succession of proper names, Ts'in-Shi Huang Ti, Hui Yuan, Chu-Hi . . . Phidias, Polygnotos, Asklepios . . . Herodotos, Plutarch, Dio Cassius, and so on. Thanks to this simple scheme Sjöstrand could complete the poem in such an amazingly short time, allowing the names that spontaneously presented themselves in his mind while writing to stand for whole periods and aspects of cultural development. Appropriately enough, many of the names belong to historians and chroniclers, some of whom Sjöstrand happened to have been reading at that time.

In his brief commentary to "Burning Alphabet," Sjöstrand claims to have adopted prominent features of Ligeti's music: "The billowing planes of sound recur in the structure of the poem, the billowing, flowing motions which are subject to vehement interruptions, voices and cries that barely rise above the waters of anonymity. A division into different contrasting blocks, as in Ligeti's third movement, also recurs in the poem."[39] This division is clearly visible on the printed page where "blocks" of five to ten lines are separated from each other by blanks. The voices and cries of the music are the capitalized names of the text, standing out from the surrounding. This technique as well as the whole tone of "Burning Alphabet" may, however, also owe something to Ekelöf's poem *A Mölna Elegy* (1960).

Sjöstrand emphasizes the liquid character of the music, speaking of billowing waters. It is an interpretation which must be said to have some foundation in the acoustic qualities of the music, not only in the poet's obsession with the element of water. The water symbolism of "Burning Alphabet" is both overt and hidden. It perhaps does not spring to the reader's mind that the Appius Claudius mentioned in the poem as Roman consul caused the first aqueduct of Rome to be built about the year 300 before Christ, nor that Frontinus held the office of "curator aquarum" and wrote a treatise called *De Aquis Urbis Romae*. But no doubt it is thanks to their watery connections that they were included in the poem as representatives of the discipline of Roman civilization which held the supply of water under firm control, as it held the waters of the unconscious soul in control by its insistence on Stoic virtues and civic duties.

One passage overtly concerned with the element of water contains, according to Sjöstrand himself, an allusion to Keats:

> But the garden where the nightingale sang The Great Flood
>   has inundated:
> Those who were drawn under the Bell to the water of madness
>   other waters
> have shrouded in burning and cold silence—

Keats's "Ode to a Nightingale" made an early and deep impression on Sjöstrand, in particular the famous lines, "Charm'd magic casements, opening on the foam / Of perilous seas, in faery lands forlorn." These perilous seas Sjöstrand associates with the waters of the soul, rising, inundating the terra firma of the conscious mind, making the position of the poet—the bird in the garden—precarious. Without the water, no poetry; but unchecked it turns into the "water of madness." This is no doubt a very personal interpretation of Keats's notoriously enigmatic lines, but the allusion cannot be doubted. The Bell, too, comes from the Ode, immediately after the lines quoted: "Forlorn! the very word is like a bell. . . ." However, a more obvious source of this imagery is the legend of the Engulfed Cathedral, which as we have seen forms a recurrent theme in Sjöstrand's poetry. It should also be added that the "madness" connected with the bell refers to a singularly cruel method of torture employed in old China of which Sjöstrand read as a boy. The fettered victim was placed under a huge bell, and submerged in its mighty sound he became mentally deranged from the sheer excess of acoustic stimulation.

The allusions to Appius Claudius, to Frontinus, and to Keats's Ode reveal an important aspect of the structure of "Burning Alphabet." It was written in one long sweep without conscious premeditation, which of necessity entails a rather straightforward structure. But within the overall structure of historical progression, we have discovered an infrastructure of subtle allusions, a network of symbols and motifs. Here, too, Ligeti's *Requiem* affords a parallel. As indicated in the summary of that composition, Ligeti has indulged in an extremely elaborate part-writing—the choruses are sometimes divided into twenty separate parts moving in accordance with strict contrapuntal rules. All these subtleties cannot, of course, be heard even by a trained professional's ear. They combine into a closely woven web of sound which is perceived only as a whole. But the effect of the whole depends upon the intricate details, in Ligeti's mass as well as in Sjöstrand's poem.

The parallel must not be pushed too far, however. Ligeti worked on his composition for two years, Sjöstrand on his for twenty minutes. For Ligeti's highly conscious and intellectual method of composing we must, in Sjöstrand's case, substitute the automatic operation of his subconscious. The materials and products of a long period of reading, pondering, feeling, and thinking were suddenly crystallized, and the hidden structures and connections in the poem were hidden to the poet himself while writing. On investigation it appears that several of the Greek names which at first sight seem picked at random have something in common. Trofonio's oracle as well as many of the historical persons referred to are all drawn from the same source, Pausanias's *Description of Greece*. This was no deliberate device of the poet's, it just so happened that he had been reading Pausanias with great interest for some time, and in the dreamlike state of writing the poem these names just appeared.[40]

Similarly with one of the most cryptic passages of the poem:

EIDOLON I read: An image of man: the Shadow's serpent:
A butterfly, a bird—

See, with an elephant head, with a body like an armadillo
    rises MAKARA MAKARA MAKABRA KADABRA—Wisdom's
    shape rises PRAJNAPARAMITA

The words MAKARA etcetera seem sheer nonsense and are
intended to illustrate the breakdown of language so prominent
in Ligeti's *Requiem* where the words of the mass are deliberately
cut to pieces. But they are not just any nonsense. As variations
on the words abracadabra and macabre they have a secret meaning, emphasized by the images of serpent, bird, elephant head,
and armadillo. These animals all bear distinctive similarities to
the figure of Abraxas, a demon in Gnostic speculation identified
with God himself, and abracadabra is thought to be a distortion
of the name Abraxas.[41] Memories of pictorial representations of
this figure combined with the idea that as abracadabra is the
same as Abraxas, so utter nonsense may be the highest wisdom—
Prajnaparamita refers to the supreme intelligence in Indian
philosophy. The meaning of the whole passage would seem to
be that the mystery of man, appearing as macabre nonsense to
those not initiated, lies in his dual nature of beast and god.

Returning to the general character of Ligeti's mass and
Sjöstrand's poem, an important difference must be stressed.
Ligeti's work is one of utter pessimism, a lamentation without
hope. It is "the end of the world." Sjöstrand, on the other hand,
though heaping historical instances of man's unfathomable cruelty
to man, is not without hope. As we shall see in the last chapter,
he foresees crises, revolutions, and catastrophes in the near
future, but he still believes in the continuation of mankind on
earth, even dreams of a new era of peace and good will. And so,
while at the end of Ligeti's *Requiem* the human voices of the
chorus are silenced in despair, the poet's last words in "Burning
Alphabet" are "I continue":

The Book is opened. There is written all the good, all the
    evil in life pursued by men.
        I know: I possess nothing.

But, with a stranger's gaze, with the eyes of a sleepwalker
on this unknown planet, I move onward from letter to
letter in the sought, the found alphabet: I have won
through to syntax: I form my first sentence:
I continue

V *In the Beginning*

The advent of electrophonic music has opened up quite new
possibilities of combining and interrelating music and literature.
The creative activity in this field, however, has not yet reached
beyond initial experimenting with different technical procedures.
For instance, an opera occasionally using synthetic electronic
sounds to accompany the voices of human singers was produced
with considerable success in Stockholm in 1958 (and later in
many places abroad), namely, Karl Birger Blomdahl's *Aniara*,
the libretto of which is a dramatic version, made by Erik Lindegren, of Harry Martinson's science-fiction epic with the same
name. But Sven-Erik Bäck has brought the integration of poetry
and music one step further by using electromagnetic recordings
of human voices chanting or reading poetry as raw material in an
electrosynthetic composition of great effect. Its name is *In
Principio* and it is built on and around two texts, the first five
verses of the Gospel of St. John and a poem by Sjöstrand.

The original idea of the work was Bäck's.[42] A religious man,
he is in the habit of reading the Bible and meditating on scriptural passages, often with a view to their musical possibilities.
So he conceived the idea of treating the central Christian utterance of St. John in a very special way. First, he availed himself
of a Greek visitor to Sweden supposed to be able to reproduce
the biblical passage in question roughly the way it was pronounced at the time it was written. He made this man record
his reading of the Greek text on tape and then proceeded to make
an acoustical analysis of the recording, using the resulting figures
for pitch, rhythm, etc., to program the electrophonic synthesizer.
But he also wished to have another, contrasting voice, reading
a text which he vaguely imagined as a modern equivalent of the
prologue to the Gospel of St. John, and that is where Östen
Sjöstrand became involved in the project. Bäck explained his

ideas and asked him to write a poem suiting these ends. It was a request that immediately stirred Sjöstrand's creative powers and in a short time he completed the poem "In Principio," first published in the spring of 1970 in the journal *Contemporary Music* together with an introductory note on the music by the composer himself.[43]

In this note Bäck points to two works which in different ways subject a poet's words to analytico-synthetic treatment similar to what he attempts in his composition. One is Pierre Boulez's *Le marteau sans maître* (1954), based on poems by René Char which, incidentally, have been translated into Swedish by Sjöstrand who also has devoted an essay to Char.[44] The other work preceding and stimulating Bäck is Witlod Lutoslavsky's *Paroles tissées*, and the words "woven" into this composition were written by the French poet Chabrun. However new-fangled the techniques employed in these works may seem, Bäck says, the underlying idea is very old:

To let texts direct musical events, and vice versa, was for instance done as early as Obrecht's time. Or, to mention earlier names: the French Pleiad poets around Ronsard had other, very advanced theories of how to merge poetry and music. But in one respect the word-note problem has really got a new solution, *i.e.* through electronics and loudspeakers. Text-sound composers say that poetry has finally come home. For myself, I would say the same thing by parodying a text which I have used in an electronic composition, *In Principio,* "verbum caro factum est." By that I mean that texts now more than ever before can be made into musical material, if we still wish to speak in such terms. . . . Utilizing vocoder, different kinds of filters and modulators, etc., I have succeeded in distilling—and composing in—the different, to my perception purely musical elements contained in the micro-world of rhythms, melodies, spectra, and formants which all the time function in the language with . . . abstract, decisive means.

The intentions and techniques set forth in this note were known to Sjöstrand in principle when he agreed to write a poem on the theme of "In the Beginning," and he responded to the requirements by writing a comparatively short and simple piece in which every line and every phrase has the ring of a natural utterance conveying an important message. The straightforward simplicity of the poem, so suitable to Bäck's musical ends, does not, however, exclude a dramatic structure and a rich symbolism. The poem is given here in its entirety, for once both in Swedish and English:

> I begynnelsen—
> I begynnelsen—
>
> då jorden var kall, eller varm
> (bara för att den rörde sig)
>
> I begynnelsen—
> I begynnelsen—
>
> innan stenen slipades
> innan händer höjdes mot en gren
>
> I begynnelsen—
> I begynnelsen—
>
> innan en skyddsdräkt var nödvändig
> mot virusmolnen, och mot elden
>
> I begynnelsen—
>
> innan skyddande och stängande murar
> restes—
>
> före alla ringmurar
>   fästningsvallar
>   skyddsvärn
>   barriärer
> före skiljeväggar, skiljemurar—
>
> innan berget, och stålet, och betongen
>   rämnade
>   sprängdes
>   sprang itu
>
> innan människor blev varse varandra
>   för första gången—
>
> alla öknar, all vildmark, alla ödelagda
>   tillflyktsorter—

stapplande, nattblinda steg mot bostäder
och städer, som reser sig ur askan—
                mot gränser, mot fronter
                som stinker av lik...

                I begynnelsen
                fanns ingen
                utom du—

                Ensamma stjärnor—
                En gemensam horisont.

                In the beginning—
                In the beginning—

when the earth was cold, or hot
(simply because it was moving)

                In the beginning—
                In the beginning—

before the stone was ground
before hands were raised towards a branch

                In the beginning—
                In the beginning—

before protective clothing was necessary
against virus clouds and fire

                In the beginning—

before defensive and enclosing walls
were raised

before all ringwalls
                ramparts
                breastworks
                barriers
before the dividing-walls and masonry—

before the rock, the steel and the concrete
                split
                exploded
                and burst

before men grew aware of each other
for the first time—

all deserts, all wildernesses, all barren
places of refuge—

tottering, night-blind steps towards dwellings
and towns rising from the ash—
towards frontiers, towards fronts
reeking of carrion . . .

In the beginning—
there was no one
except you—

Solitary stars——
A common horizon.

The time span covered by these 37 lines is the whole of terrestrial existence, from the formation of the still lifeless planet up to the present time and perhaps even beyond it. The images of ruined towns rising out of their ashes may refer to wars and disasters that have already occurred, or to future catastrophes, or both. The apex of this span and the climax of the poem is reached in the lines, "before the rock, the steel and the concrete / split / exploded / and burst." This is the ultimate phase in the development of man's mastery over nature, always used for destructive ends, which began when primitive man fashioned his first tool out of stone and culminated in the detonation of the first atomic bomb.

The poetic progression toward this detonating climax is achieved through a series of increasingly aggressive and warlike images: "ringwalls," "ramparts," "breastworks," "barriers." And Bäck's music reinforces the effect by a continuous crescendo reaching its climax shortly after the middle of the piece, *i.e.* in the beginning of the fifth minute of the eight minutes' duration of the whole composition.[45] Correspondingly, the lines "exploded / and burst" occur shortly after the middle of the poem.

The electrophonic interpretation of the opening lines also agrees with Sjöstrand's conception of the beginning of the world, not explicitly stated in this poem but to be inferred from his other writings. It is a conception in which the hypotheses of modern cosmology are bringing scientific authority to symbolic modes of representation such as those of Genesis and the Gospel of St. John. The Spirit that moves upon the face of the waters creating light, or the Word that is light shining in darkness, are symbols or expressions not very far removed from those employed by certain scientists trying to explain the scientifically inexplicable mystery of the beginning of the world and the creation of energy. The mysterious generation of energy, light, and life out of the void is perhaps better suggested in music than in words, since the physical properties of sound are in many ways analogous to those of light. And if that is so, electronic music is by its very nature more apt than traditional music, as would seem to appear from a comparison between, say, the charming naïveté of Haydn's *Creation* and the abstract intensity of Bäck's *In Principio*.

Sjöstrand is anxious to free his poem from any narrow scriptural associations. In his note to it at the end of *The Dream is No Façade* he rather emphasizes its general, psychological meaning:

In this poem which (to me) records revolt, disintegration and new interior settlements, there are of course . . . echoes of the prologue to the Gospel of St. John. But I wish to point out: the search for new creative beginnings lies deep in most men, in almost every religion. I also wish to emphasize that the key words of the poem are, "before men grew aware of each other / for the first time." This (final) departure for the future which is living with us, is associated with the concluding lines "Solitary stars— / A common horizon."

The turning point in life—individual or social—as well as in history occurs when man becomes aware of his neighbor and fellowman as a person like himself. Then, Sjöstrand would seem to say and hope, aggression, destruction, and war may be replaced by a common creative effort. The stress he lays on creativity in the note just quoted is natural enough in a poem treating the beginning of the world, but it is not the unique creation of the universe in a past beyond all time and comprehension that concerns him here. It is rather the continuous creation, in the physical

as well as in the biological and spiritual senses of the term. Sjöstrand's view of creativeness as the sign of the dignity of man, the
homo dei, has been considered in the previous chapter, and the
general ideas discussed there all have a bearing on "In Principio."

Returning to Bäck's music, the vocal material he used is barely
discernible in the first half of the composition. Of the Greek
words of the Gospel only a few are heard as words: en archæ ho
lógos (In the beginning the word). And of Sjöstrand's poem,
read by himself, it is only the final five lines that come across as
a verbal message. But before words begin to take on shape and
meaning they are heard as fragments, as phonetic particles
which, technically, are mere acoustic phenomena but yet recog-
nizable as particles of human speech. It is one of Bäck's great
achievements in *In Principio* that he so clearly and dramatically
pictures the gradual emergence of speech and language in the
evolutionary process. Behind this process lies, in his belief, the
Word, the original creative Logos of Genesis and St. John, and
when, toward the end of the composition, the poet's voice is
heard to utter distinct words, that means that the divine Word
after eons of inarticulate life-giving finally has found a mouth-
piece in spiritually creative man. And this is a new beginning.
This treatment of the poet's words gives him an almost Christ-like
function as the Word incarnate—an idea far from new in the
history of Romantic genius. But to Bäck and Sjöstrand it is both
something more and something less at stake than the Romantic
idea of the divine seer. Declining all pretentions of the exceptional genius, they rather wish to point to what is, or could
and ought to be, common to all men. If this is a heresy, it is
one of which Christ himself was accused according to one of
Sjöstrand's favorite Scripture sayings, "Is it not written in your
law, I said, Ye are gods? If he called them gods, unto whom the
word of God came..." (John, X: 34 f.).

This brief theological note is necessary in order to appreciate
the meaning of the last five lines and Bäck's treatment of them.
His reference to Obrecht and his time, quoted above, indicates
not only a historical interest in the early phases of church music
but also a preoccupation with the more esoteric aspects of composing. In the sixteenth century music was still considered more

a branch of mathematics than of the fine arts, and the numerical speculation involved in writing music was often extended to the sacred texts used. The equation of letters with numbers was well established in the cabalistic and eschatologic tradition. In the spirit of this tradition Bäck set out to manipulate the concluding lines of Sjöstrand's poem, using the Word itself as a code. In Greek the name Christ is, of course, spelled with seven letters, CH-R-I-S-T-O-S. The holy number of seven is further associated with Christ's Seven Words on the Cross. And finally, the concluding lines of "In Principio" are, the way Bäck reads them, made up of seven words: (1) In the beginning; (2) there was; (3)no one; (4) except you; (5) solitary stars; (6) a common; (7) horizon. The order in which these seven "words" are repeated in Bäck's composition is calculated on the alphabetical order of the separate letters of the name Christos according to a code too complicated to be explained here in detail. As a result, the following sequence of words is heard when, toward the end of the piece, the verbal content of the poet's utterance becomes clearly discernible: horizon, except you, common, solitary, there was, solitary stars, horizon, no one, a common, in the beginning, in the beginning, except you, no one, there was, common. The first of these words are reproduced very softly, almost as a whisper. The following form a crescendo up to the second "horizon" after which the sound of both speaker and music gradually falls down to a few, soft, thin notes accompanying the last word, common. By putting that word at the very end, Bäck of course strongly emphasizes the social, anti-individualistic, "democratic" creed of the poem.

It is doubtful how much of this musical interpretation can be considered relevant to the poetic text as such. The number symbolism, for instance, was clearly not intended by Sjöstrand, although he had used the Seven Words with symbolic reference to the creative Logos in one of the poems in *Consecration*.[46]

Otherwise, Bäck's reading seems fully warranted by the text. The "you" that was in the beginning can be none other than the Word of God, but it is not capitalized and can also be any man, including the poet: for each individual being, the world begins with self-consciousness. To itself, each ego is a solitary star shining in darkness, but the horizon is common to all, as all men partake of the common conditions of human existence.

The last two lines of "In Principio" are fraught with deep symbolic significance to Sjöstrand, so much so that, bringing out a selection of his poetry in 1970, he gave it the title *Solitary Stars, a Common Horizon.*

CHAPTER 3

Poetry and Science

I *The "Two Cultures"*

ONE of the reasons for the unfortunate dichotomy of the "two cultures" seems to be linguistic. The English word *science*, originally meaning learning and knowledge in general, is of course now restricted to such systematized bodies of knowledge as are founded on the data of so-called objective observations to the exclusion of introspective, emotional, or purely intellectual experience. Other languages, German and Swedish for example, have a corresponding word of wider implication; *Wissenschaft*, in Swedish *vetenskap*, covers any system of knowledge, whether based on scientific data or scholarly research. History is as much of a *vetenskap* as physics, esthetics as much as biology. There was a time at the beginning of the nineteenth century when Swedish poetry, humanities, and science alike were dominated by a common view of the world derived from German Romantic idealism. Scientific speculation merged with the philosophy of history and art, and poetry was considered not only a suitable means of expressing the grand syntheses arrived at but an instrument or faculty of knowledge in its own right. There are traces of such Romantic views in Sjöstrand's work— some were pointed out above in dealing with his ideas of inspiration and creativity—and as we shall presently see, one of the foundations of his elemental symbolism is to be found in the great Swedish Romantic poet E. J. Stagnelius.

There is a limit to the power of words, however. The triumphant progress of "objective" science since the middle of the nineteenth century obliterated the Romantic dream of a unified *vetenskap*, and in the ensuing war between scientific, materialistic positivism and transcendental idealism, poetry generally sided with idealism, though in the development from Symbolism to

Modernism the transcendental element was often replaced by psychological qualities. To the extent that science became synonymous with knowledge based on observations of material objects, poetry and science appeared mutually exclusive. The whole world of values, emotions, philosophical speculation, and religious aspiration was, logically enough, banned from the realm of positivistic science, and since science often came to be identified with truth, many scientists tended to look upon the other world as fantasy and fiction, harmless when in the guise of art and poetry but a vicious enemy when revealing its superstitious nature in religion and metaphysics.

Of course such crude polemics now belong to the past, but that does not mean that the gap is bridged, as the topicality of C. P. Snow's analysis of the "two cultures" clearly shows. For many decades, however, there has accumulated evidence of growing impatience among scientists with the smug claims of their branches of learning to explain, and explain away, the mysteries of life and the universe. For example, the problem of what constitutes organic life now seems to require as much philosophical consideration as experimental research, and the study of elementary particles has dissolved the traditional concept of matter itself and thrown the physicists back upon a critical examination of the primary concepts and ideas of their own science. And it appears that such considerations and critical examinations tend to involve the scientist himself as experimenter, observer, and interpreter.

It no longer seems tenable that there is an objective world that can be studied without reference to the nature and mental constitution of the student. It has long been tacitly assumed that in science everything can be reduced to quantities and figures; qualitative experience is subjective, unverifiable, and hence irrelevant, at best a secondary epiphenomenon, at worst a mere illusion. Now this view is becoming equally untenable. The qualitative experience of, say, different colors is as real and primary as the quantitative data of wavelengths and frequencies and demands recognition as a legitimate field of scientific inquiry. But it must be granted that such an inquiry should include the human mind itself, as the instrument whereby colors are experienced qualitatively, whereas spectroscopes only measure the quantities of wavelengths. This question of colors forms a good illustration of the dilemma of modern science and, besides, it enters into the subject matter of one of the Sjöstrand poems to be discussed below.

The inclusion of the scientist and his mind in the field of scientific research can obviously be taken as a sign of reconciliation between science and the humanities. Arthur Koestler, one of the most talented popularizers of recent developments in scientific thought, and one whom Sjöstrand has read with great interest, puts the case somewhat arrogantly: "It is embarrassing to have to repeat, over and again, that two half-truths do not make a truth, and two half-cultures do not make a culture. Science cannot provide the ultimate answers...."[1] In biology Koestler sees the tendencies toward integration as mere "threads of ideas trailing on the fringes of orthodoxy"[2] but in physics several outstanding thinkers have emphatically detached themselves from prevalent positivistic notions. Einstein, as is well known, defended the idea of a purposefully ordered cosmos of natural laws when, in response to the statistical theory of electrons, he refused to believe that the Good Lord plays at dice. It is not the occasional reference to a divine order that is significant here, however, but the emphasis on the human aspects of science. An eloquent plea for this is delivered by Erwin Schrödinger in his book *Science and Humanism*:

You may ask...: What, then, is in your opinion the value of natural science? I answer: Its scope, aim and value is the same as that of any other branch of human knowledge. Nay, none of them alone, only the union of them all, has any scope or value at all, and that is simply enough described: it is to obey the command of the Delphic deity,... Get to know yourself. Or, to put it in the brief, impressive rhetoric of Plotinus (*Enn.* VI, 4, 14):... "And we, who are we anyhow?" He continues: "Perhaps we were *there* already before this creation came into existence, human beings of another type, or even some sort of gods, pure souls and mind united with the whole universe, parts of the intelligible world, not separated and cut off, but at one with the whole."[3]

It would be difficult to find a statement by an authoritative physicist more pertinent to the poetry of Östen Sjöstrand.

It is all very well that scientists stretch out their hands to their brothers in the humanities, but it is often difficult for the other party to grasp that hand owing to sheer lack of knowledge. For one thing, the pattern of the "two cultures" has successfully established itself in the educational system, making it almost impossible to obtain, while at school, both a solid grounding in the classics and a not altogether superficial orientation in modern science. And without proper schooling authors tend to pick up isolated concepts and catchwords and apply them completely out of context, as in the case of Lawrence Durrell's attempt to relate Einsteinian relativity to fiction.[4] Of course even a wholly self-taught man may grasp the essentials of advanced scientific thought, as indicated by the Swedish poet Harry Martinson in his cosmic epic poem *Aniara* (1956). Sjöstrand's case is an intermediary one. He has no academic training but at high school he opted for a scientific course, and what he learned there was strongly reinforced and expanded through his contact with the oceanographer and physicist Professor Hans Pettersson, mentioned in a previous chapter. Most important in this informal training was the acquisition of the habit of seeing things from a scientific point of view and not being scared away by technical jargon and mathematical formulas. And he learned to move with intellectual ease among the most recent scientific discoveries and theories—for instance, when the first atomic bomb was dropped in 1945 he could discuss the occasion with the author of the first Swedish book on nuclear fission.[5] He has continued to keep himself informed of the vanguard research by regularly reading publications such as *Nature* and a variety of books summing up and analyzing the position at the frontiers of astronomy, physics, and biology.

Of Sjöstrand's—equally unacademic—education in theology and the humanities something was said in Chapter 1, and it seems that he, on his level of learning, would be exceptionally well equipped to achieve a successful integration of the "two cultures" in his poetic work. The scientific elements in his poetry are obvious even to a casual reader. Titles such as "Fade-Outs," "Memory Quanta," "Orbits, Thoroughfares," and "The Study of Stress" catch the eye of the poetry reader not used to that kind of subject matter, and phrases like "radiation belts" and "wandering magnetic fields" startle in a poem devoted to Wisdom as the poet's muse. The word quanta in "Memory Quanta,"[6] however, is no mere decoration but a means of conveying an experience of the function of *creative memory*: not a continuous reel to be played back at will but a spontaneous presentation to the mind's eye of whole clusters, as it were, of imagery; and the best way of conveying this experience seemed to be an analogy to the discontinuous behavior of microcosmic matter and energy.

More important than the metaphoric use of scientific terms are the wider ideas and theories derived from science that have molded the very conception of whole poems. It often takes a detailed analysis of the poetic text to reveal the underlying theory, which is never an end in itself but a pattern for ordering human experience. The commentaries on some representative poems that follow later in this chapter may invite the misunderstanding that Sjöstrand's use of scientific imagery and theories is highly studied, the outcome of laborious reading and intellectual deliberation. Nothing could be wider of the mark, however. The reading may be both deliberate and laborious, but once accomplished it directs the creative process from the unconscious layers of the poet's mind. Since this process is inaccessible to analysis, the literary critic must confine himself to more objective evidence, *i.e.*, to a comparison of the finished poem with such literature as Sjöstrand may have or avowedly has read.

Now, Sjöstrand's scientific imagination is not solely nourished by the highly advanced theories of recent decades. It was mentioned above that he has also immersed himself in the speculation of the Romantics, and in this connection we should now examine some further aspects of his water symbolism.

II *Elements, Matter, and Mind*

Sjöstrand's preoccupation with elemental symbolism, particularly water, has already been demonstrated in several different contexts: the elements appeared to indicate inner, psychological qualities, and water Sjöstrand constantly associates with music and the unconscious. Though the accents of his symbolism are highly personal, the symbolism itself is firmly rooted in poetic tradition, and insofar as it has anything to do with science, it would seem to be with those types of ancient Greek science that reduced everything to one or a few primordial elements and later via alchemy and the Hermetic teachings entered the natural philosophy of the Renaissance and the Romantic era. Much in Sjöstrand's work can be accounted for by referring it to that tradition, as we shall presently see, but it will also appear that he has gone beyond it in an attempt to link it with modern science.

A good starting point for this discussion is the following short poem from *Consecration*, to which Sjöstrand attaches special importance—he reprinted it in a later book of otherwise original poems:

> The mirror at the bottom of the pail.
> Stillness in that which was and is to be.
> The moment's dependence.
>
> Midnight's motionless face—
> and the island vanishing in dark space.[7]

There is a wealth of ideas and allusions condensed into those five lines. The central image is that of a reflection in water, the reflection of the starry sky—"Midnight's motionless face"—and the vanishing island is of course Atlantis, a variation on Sjöstrand's favorite theme of the Engulfed Cathedral. Between the reflection and the reflected, between the depths of water and the lights of heaven, between the soul of man and the divine, there prevails a correspondence which can be experienced only in a moment of mystic union, "the moment's dependence," a moment "in and out of time," to use T. S. Eliot's phrase, a moment in which are gathered past and future, "that which was and is to be."

This mystical element in the poem can be clarified further by referring to an essay which Sjöstrand wrote in the same year as the poem. There he identifies the meaning of "the mirror at the bottom of the pail" with Meister Eckhart's "Seelenfünklein," with the *scintilla*, the "little spark of the soul" of that

German mystic whom he studied at the time.[8] The reference to Eckhart gives substance to the mystical interpretation but also invites occult associations. C. G. Jung finds Eckhart's *scintilla* identical with the point where, in the teachings of classical alchemy, the elemental opposites meet and unite. In the poem the opposites are of course water and heavenly fire, and in Jung's psychological interpretation "water in all its forms—sea, lake, river, spring—is one of the commonest typifications of the unconscious,"[9] while fire, light, gold are common symbols of the divine, whether as a transcendental deity or an immanent quality in man.

Within the occult tradition the elements often stand for two kinds of reality, physical and psychical. Fire, air, water, and earth are the elements out of which the material world is built but they are also elements of the soul. This duality is neither a matter of confusion, nor of contradiction, for at the root of this tradition lies the conception of the material world as an outflow from the supreme spirit, who manifests itself on different levels; on the lowest level as matter, on a higher as soul or mind. Before Sjöstrand acquainted himself with Jung's psychological theories of elemental symbolism he had encountered something very similar in the poetry of E. J. Stagnelius (1793–1823). In a manner not unlike that of William Blake, Stagnelius constructed a mythology of his own on materials from the Gnostic Christian tradition, and in a set of four poems called "The Elements" he tells the esoteric story of how primordial Fire was enticed to union with that "guileful bride," Water, who conceived and brought forth their daughter, Earth.[10] In accordance with the Gnostic teachings Stagnelius considers the elemental union, out of which the physical world is born, a fall into sin and mortality, and the association of the fall with sexual union is essential.

This esoteric speculation may seem to have taken us far away from Sjöstrand's relation to modern science, but there is a psychological connection worth dwelling upon. In the occult doctrine of the elements he found a foreshadowing of the idea of correspondence or identity between the soul and the world which, in utterly different terms, has come to the fore in current scientific speculation. Moreover, the association in that occult doctrine of the elemental union with fall, sin, and sexuality seems strongly to have moved the adolescent poet striving to reconcile his natural and spiritual urges. The Gnostic way of salvation leads through "gnosis," through knowledge of the origin and nature of the world and the soul back to the ultimate knowledge of God, the One. In the emotional thinking of the young poet, science, the exploration of the natural world, came to appear as a second road to salvation and knowledge of God, the first being the direct vision and mystic union. This, of course, is nothing but the old medieval doctrine of the twofold revelation: in Christ the Word and in the Book of Nature. It is a long way from the excited speculations of the twenty-year-old Sjöstrand to the more cautious and sober ventures of the mature poet into the realm of modern physics—as long a way as that from ancient gnosis to contemporary philosophy of science. But it is a continuous road in both cases, and some of the milestones in the development of physical thought are also pertinent to the development of Sjöstrand's thinking.

The roots of elemental science are of course to be found among the so called pre-Socratic philosophers who advanced theories of a separate element as the ultimate substance of material existence, water, air, fire as the case might be. Most influential among them was Heraclitus—"Heraclitus, the Enigmatic," as Sjöstrand called a set of poetic fragments published in a literary review in 1949.[11] He was attracted by the Greek philosopher's insistence on change as the fundamental quality of existence. At the root of all things is fire, Heraclitus teaches, the everlasting fire, but its chief secondary manifestation is water which by its fluid instability reveals its descent from the true element of change. "Panta rei" "everything is in a flux," is perhaps Heraclitus's best known aphorism, further developed in his saying that we can never step into the same river twice—in the meantime the water flows and we change. Sjöstrand also attempts some comparisons between Heraclitus and more modern philosophers, Spinoza, Hegel, and Bergson. In particular Bergson fits into Sjöstrand's Heraclitean pattern of thought: "la durée," duration or real, inner time, is pictured by Bergson as a river of creative evolution.

In these early fragments Sjöstrand interprets Heraclitus in terms of common human philosophy, but as he later immersed himself in modern physics he found that Heraclitus had foreshadowed central ideas in contemporary science. Werner Heisenberg for instance, concerning himself with the Heraclitean doctrine of fire, writes:

This leads to the antithesis of Being and Becoming and finally to the solution of Heraclitus, that the change itself is the fundamental principle, the "imperishable change that renovates the world," as the poets have called it. But the change in itself is not a material cause and therefore is represented in the philosophy of Heraclitus by the fire as the basic element, which is both matter and a moving force.

We may remark at this point that modern physics is in some way extremely near to the doctrines of Heraclitus. If we replace the word "fire" by the word "energy" we can almost repeat his statements word for word from our modern point of view.[12]

Heraclitus's insights into the structure of the natural world were not limited to its physical aspects, however. In the concept of God or the Logos he expressed the intuition that behind the eternal change and war between opposites lies unity. Behind the world of appearance lies transcendent mind—that chief tenet of philosophical idealism has for some time been tentatively creeping back into the thinking of modern physicists, thus drawing them even closer to Heraclitus. Sjöstrand seems to hint at this aspect of Heraclitus when he puts his name beside Spinoza's, adding the equation, "logos—deus sive natura."[13]

The idea of reducing the world to fundamental elements uniting in opposition makes Heraclitus something of a forerunner of Hegel, too—the youthful philosopher Sjöstrand suggests this perhaps not altogether convincing equation, "Heraclitus—Hegel: poetic truth as against political truth."[14] But Heraclitus's war of opposites can also be interpreted as a poetic statement of the modern view of matter as a sort of synthesis of opposing charges of energy. And this thought becomes prominent in Sjöstrand's later poetry, where terms such as "counter-statements" and "counter-images"[15] testify to his need for the balancing of opposites. Referring to Heraclitus in his 1967 collection, he makes balance in tension and union of opposites the very essence of poetry: "Attunement of opposing tensions, like that of the bow and the lyre."[16] Bow and lyre were both attributes of Apollo, the god of poetry.

The harmony derived from the tension of the stringed lyre is a common enough poetic metaphor which surely needs no scientific explanation. But it seems that Sjöstrand interprets it in the light of nuclear physics, for in that same collection he writes of Wisdom:

> She led me over
> the decisive threshold—to the Poem,
> thermonuclear energy,
> the liberated Common Spirit . . .[17]

Here poetry is frankly equated with the as yet unexplained energy or force that holds together the separate parts of the atomic nucleus, a force whose polarities are similar to those of electrical and magnetic forces and which achieves by such balancing of opposites the kind of stability and harmony we recognize in terms of matter. When Sjöstrand declares Poetry to be the same thing as this energy, he is not indulging in a taste for fanciful metaphors but repeats a central idea in Romantic idealism according to which spirit and matter are outflows from the same common source and hence structurally alike and Poetry, in an absolute sense and with capital P, the supreme means of knowing and revealing the fundamental identity of the material and the spiritual world. What separates Sjöstrand from the Romantics is that they built their speculation on very vague and fanciful conceptions of matter and energy as components of the physical world, whereas he has access to scientific discoveries which exceed the wildest hopes of the Romantics. To put it in a somewhat provocative way: modern science, far from refuting the natural philosophy of the idealist tradition, has given it substance and validity—not in all its aspects and consequences, of course, but in its insistence on the derivative character of the material world and on the unity of the underlying principle, be it called mind, spirit, God, or something else. In the poem quoted above it is called Wisdom:

"Before the depths I was,
before the dust condensed,
the least elements were split, I was
in the thinking matter
as the Gate to creation..."

The line of thought followed in this poem is by no means
foreign to leading modern physicists, as Erwin Schrödinger
clearly demonstrates in his book *Mind and Matter*. Discussing
the problem of subjective experience and objective knowledge,
he speaks of the "hypothesis of the real world around us."
"Without being aware of it and without being rigorously systematic about it, we exclude the Subject of Cognizance from the
domain of nature that we endeavour to understand. We step with
our own person back into the part of an onlooker who does not
belong to the world, which by this very procedure becomes an
objective world."[18] This attitude to reality leads, he holds, to
"blatant antinomies," one of which is the discrimination between
subject and object, between mind and matter. In order to resolve
it Schrödinger suggests that we go to the source of all transcendent idealism, to the Upanishads and their doctrine of the
oneness of mind as the ultimate reality:

Still, it must be said that to Western thought this doctrine has little
appeal, it is unpalatable, it is dubbed fantastic, unscientific. Well, so
it is, because our science—Greek science—is based on objectivation,
whereby it has cut itself off from an adequate understanding of the
Subject of Cognizance, of the mind. But I do believe that this is
precisely the point where our present way of thinking does need
to be amended, perhaps by a bit of blood-transfusion from Eastern
thought.[19]

Examples of such blood transfusions in Sjöstrand's poetry will be
discussed later in this chapter.

In order to return to the starting-point, we may now read the
line, "The mirror at the bottom of the pail," as a comprehensive
statement of the relation between divine oneness and the individual soul—a relation which includes the whole cosmic world—
"Midnight's motionless face"—in its entire temporal extension

and which illustrates the elemental opposition, here between fire and water, that is the essence of reality.

III Deep-Sea Psychology

Water as the element of the unconscious has of course become a cliché in much post-Freudian poetry, and it takes something special to make the symbol interesting and poetically effective these days. Sjöstrand's contribution is original enough: in his early work he achieves some startling results by using oceanography as a source of imagery and terminology. Not that he was hunting for originality. As a member, more or less, of Professor Hans Pettersson's household the jargon of oceanography came naturally to him, and during his visits to the oceanographic station outside Gothenburg in the 1940's he had some first-hand experience of the scientific techniques used in deep-sea research:

I learned about echo sounding, sedimentation and Kullenberg's coring tube at about the same time as I began reading my first William books in English. Oceanography formed a regular ingredient of summer pastimes. After climbing the hills of Bornö, after stealthily watching the deer come out of the wood to drink at dusk, we would hurry down to the oceanographic station, wind up Nansen bottles out of the Gullmar Fjord, log entries of salinity, temperature, and depth. On a moving cylinder a pen traced the submarine waves far below in the depths of the fjord.[20]

This is the personal background of a set of poems in *Consecration* saturated with oceanographic imagery. The *Challenger*, one of the first oceanographic research vessels, is invoked in one poem, and free use is made of terms such as abyssal sediments, white ooze, red clay, manganese nodules, all of which are fully explained in Pettersson's popular books *Oceanography* and *The Enigmas of the Deep Sea*.[21]

It is a world of mystery and darkness that Sjöstrand conjures up, a world where "No corals or pearls / crown the seabed craters," where "All time is extinguished, all sunrises mute."[22] The corals and pearls are of course allusions to Ariel's song in *The Tempest*, but the sea changes suffered deep down in "azoic Winters"[23] are more metaphysical than poetical.

One of the poems, written in the characteristic five-line· form, is on the literal level a paraphrase of Pettersson's text book account:[24]

Sunk in dark rest: manganese clumps,
planetary movements in fossil layers,
hardened drips of meteors, ear bones of whales.

All the life cycles, with their eyes, are motionless, dispersed:
before the seal of the light years is broken by the tone wave
of a thought.[25]

That which is sunk in dark rest is the sedimentation on the bottom of the oceans, deep down where no light penetrates. There lie clumps of manganese formed by the enormous pressure of miles of water, and calcium remains from animals. And the stratification of these pelagic deposits reflects the history of the earth, the cyclic changes in its motion and the violent catastrophes: dislocations, volcanic eruptions, and ice ages. Everything is recorded in the abyssal sedimentation which also contains elements from outer space: shooting stars submerged in the ocean, bedded on its bottom. Owing to the perpetual and complete darkness prevailing at the bottom of the oceans, the writing of this million-year historical record is invisible. It is only with the aid of instruments invented by creative thought that the "seal" of prehistory has been broken.

That is the literal meaning. Recognizing the symbolic meaning of the depths of water, however, we must attribute further qualities to the abyssal sediments. At the bottom of each soul lie the image and epitome of the whole world, a microcosm of which we are unconscious because it is sunk in perpetual darkness until the tone wave of knowledge and insight breaks the seal. This microcosmic analogy is only implicit in the poem quoted above but it is clearly stated in the following, of which only the first three lines lend themselves to poetic translation:

In the ocean of all the worlds—
In millimeter centuries we trace the seven words.
In white ooze and red clay lies the analogy of becoming.[26]

At the bottom of the sea we find not only the annals of the earth, its physical history, in that each millimeter of sedimentation corresponds to a century's events above the surface. Putting a symbolic construction upon the oceanographic imagery, we also find a record of the spiritual history of man on earth, an "analogy of becoming" and, since becoming is inevitably linked with suffering, the other analogy is the Seven Words of Christ on the Cross, the archetype, in the Western world, of human suffering. In this poem the symbolic meaning completely overshadows the literal one from the very first line: "In the ocean of all the worlds," of all worlds in time and space, inward and outward. The psychological aspect of the universal analogy is brought out in the fourth line which says that that which helps us reach rock bottom in our own souls is the recognition of the correspondence between ourselves and the universal conditions of becoming, being, and suffering. The last line elaborates the same idea. Just as the depths of the Atlantic Ocean according to the legend hides a sunken world of perfection, so the depths of the soul hide a primordial mode of blissful existence, engulfed and lost through a fall even as the Atlantides were guilty of their own downfall. But the seal may be broken, to use the image of the previous poem, the submerged riches may be lifted up into the light of the surface. This retrieval can be put in different terms: theologically, as atonement and salvation; psychologically and esthetically, as the articulation and shaping in art of vital though latent contents of the unconscious. The metapoetic meaning of the poem is emphasized by the choice of symbol for the eternal drama of suffering: the seven *words*.

Finally, an example of Sjöstrand's use of another branch of oceanography. One of Hans Pettersson's dissertations, published in English, is entitled *Scattering and Extinction of Light in Sea-Water*,[27] and the optical phenomena resulting from the refraction of light in water form the basis of the imagery in the following poem:

> motionless water
> with colors veiling near depths
> surface
> reflecting a silence

deeper than the silence
the wind has abandoned

without need of shores
but the first star of space
where can your life be[28]

The veiling of the depths by the multicolored opacity of a surface exposed to sunlight is a common experience of anyone who has watched the sun set over the ocean, but the veiling colors in the poem also refer to the variegated spectrum of the conscious mind which prevents the deeper contents of the soul from realizing themselves in consciousness.

The surface of consciousness is, in the imagery of the poem, motionless, "reflecting silence." The soul is quiet and still like the evening sea, waiting but not yet attaining the stillness of transparency. If the surface is consciousness, then the shores are that which bounds and surrounds the ego, the objective world of the senses. But the poem affirms that shores are not needed, the world of the senses is inessential, perhaps even an obstacle, to attaining that which the quiet soul is waiting for. "The first star of space," however, is necessary. The setting of the poem again seems to be evening at sea when the first star appears in the gathering dusk. It is the star that the soul has been waiting for, the star shining from above all terrestrial elements. Not until these elements and their counterparts in the soul have come to rest, can the depths receive the light from above, can the "little spark" be reunited with its source. It is perhaps this mystic union that the poet wants to express in the last line, purposely devoid of imagery and even of ordinary grammatical structure.

IV *The New Knowledge*

Stars and galaxies form an integral part of Sjöstrand's poetic imagery throughout his work, but in its early phase their scientific associations are often obscured by their radiance as heavenly lights symbolical of the eternal and the divine. The impact of astronomy and the science of time and space, so marked in his later work, is the outcome of sustained studies, but it was only slowly that the human meaning and poetic possibilities of these studies became clear to him. A poem from 1958 called "Planetary Echoes" is the first to be dominated by astronomical imagery, and not until 1967, in the book *In the Sign of Aquarius*, did Sjöstrand make science one of his chief poetic concerns. The remainder of this chapter will be devoted to a thorough discussion of two pieces from that book. The title of the first is "Den nya kunskapen," which means "The New Knowledge," or "The New Science," the second translation being somewhat free but suggestive of a philosophical work relevant to Sjöstrand's thought at that time, Giambattista Vico's *Principii di una scienza nuova d'intorno alla natura della nazioni* (1725). The more comprehensive term "knowledge" is perhaps to be preferred, though the poem was prompted by meditations on the most recent tendencies in contemporary physical science.

The New Knowledge

Photons, neutrons, protons . . . Suddenly
with the altered wavelength (in the radio telescope):
the growing discs of sun and moon. Suddenly
he leans in over the fleeing galaxies,
the prism of the colors. As in an apparition he sees
his own thoughts, his own reflection
of the face he has almost forgotten!

He thinks that he thinks . . . He thinks
in the stuff reality and dreams are woven of—
Look: the smoke rises over the city. Men
get up from breakfast table and work table . . .
A weekday's want and labor dissolves in air,
thin air—

       Like a violent swirl
through his generation's thoughts and formulae
(for the simple and the difficult) he hears
the voice he has almost forgotten and denied—

In words that (most of all) are like sand grains,
and light quanta, he senses the inner vision's paths

of light, the human hope. And discerns
just when the reflection breaks,
the vanishing contours
of himself, of the Helper, the Friend . . .

A new time's architecture will not protect us
against the darkness of the space deserts . . .

           Listen: exiled birds
are crying over the city. The sirens, on the other side of the river,
are sounding. On the dark half of the earth
men are hurrying to the night shift,
directing the radio telescopes, adjusting the wavelengths,
seeking the new formula, for the neutron's electric
and magnetic structure.

He looks at his friends, thinks:
about the light's elementary particles, the night's sun.[29]

What new knowledge is it that this poem proclaims? To put
it briefly, and for the moment only in terms of science, it is the
knowledge that in physics we do not study reality independent
of man but only reality as seen and shaped by man's perceptual
apparatus. This idea was mentioned above in passing, but the
present poem calls for further exploration. The idea must be
seen against the background of classical physics in which the
scientist was considered the objective onlooker, measuring and
experimenting with solid objects moving according to the fixed
laws of mechanics, and these objects and laws were considered,
as a matter of course, to exist wholly in their own right and together to form the world of objective reality. The place of man
in this objective world was twofold: as a physical being he belonged to the dimension of extension, to use Descartes's term,
and is as such subject to the universal laws of mechanics; but as
a perceiving and intelligent being he belonged to the dimension
of cogitation and was tacitly assumed to be removed from that
other world of physical facts, which he could observe and the
secrets of which he could explore until they would all prove
but new aspects of solid particles in lawful motion. How
those two aspects of man and reality were fitted together,
God only knew.

We must picture the protagonist of the poem, at its outset, as a scientist of the traditional school. He is pondering what is left of solid matter, *i.e.* the elementary particles, if such they be: photons, neutrons, protons; he is observing the celestial bodies in his telescope; when suddenly something upsets his scientific routine. Instead of, or rather in, the objective astronomic phenomena he believes himself to be observing, he sees a reflection of himself, of his own thoughts. Let us consider the meaning of this sudden discovery.

The full realization of the "new" knowledge and its startling consequences may well come suddenly to the individual scientist, but in the history of scientific thought it has been more a matter of growing insight, though perhaps progressing in dramatic jumps. If the classical world picture of physics is that defined by Descartes and Newton, the first questioning of it occurred already in the late eighteenth century when Kant, in his *Critique of Pure Reason*, maintained that the objective world as such, the "thing in itself," cannot be grasped by man who perceives the world through the filter of the categories and forms of his mental constitution. Far from upsetting the routine of scientific research, however, this doctrine of Kant's was readily acknowledged: scientists were happy to leave the thing in itself to the futile speculations of metaphysical philosophers; the "things for us" were real enough for them and the only legitimate field of scientific inquiry. The seed of doubt sown by Kant was buried in the overwhelming mountain of scientific facts amassed during the following century.

Kant did not pick a quarrel with the authorities of physics as did his great contemporary, Goethe, who extended the benefits of his universal genius to most fields of knowledge and research, including physics. Goethe's quarrel with Newton's theory of light and colors—he felt that Newton had explained away the essential qualitative aspect of color—is well-known and usually brushed aside as the inconsequential vagary of a mind straying from its proper realm of greatness, poetry. But as we shall soon see, Goethe's ideas on colors have recently been in some measure rehabilitated.

The real break with the classical view of the physical world as absolute, objective and self-contained was of course effected by Einstein. The general implications of his theory of relativity and of the identity of mass and energy were philosophically digested between the wars by many an eminent thinker—Whitehead, Russell, and Eddington to mention only some British names—and their task was even more complicated by the advent of quantum physics. Heisenberg's theory of indeterminacy further eroded the fundamental concepts of classical physics in that the law of mechanistic determination was replaced by the laws of statistical probability. The road to a wholly new conception of the nature of scientific knowledge lay open.

It was not only in physics, however, that such a notion was beginning to appear. Neurological and psychological investigations into the process of perception revealed a bewildering state of affairs: scientifically speaking, our perceptions are electrochemical events in the brain, often occasioned, no doubt, by events in the external world, but how and to what extent are as yet unanswered questions of profound philosophical complexity, as is shown by, among others, the prominent neurophysiologist Russell Brain in his essay "The Nature of Perception."[30] Suddenly the old problem of body and soul seemed relevant again, and today rephrased as the problem of matter and mind it occupies the thoughts of many a respectable physicist and biologist.[31] And what once seemed a wild notion of Romantic mysticism—that matter might be secondary to mind—is now a notion seriously entertained by sober philosophers of science.

Another discipline where similar lines of thought are now being pursued is linguistics. The common view of language is of course that it is a vehicle of communication between people. But comparative studies of widely different languages, such as English and certain North American Indian dialects, have focused attention on another and perhaps more fundamental aspect. Named after the two linguists and anthropologists E. Sapir and B. L. Whorf the so-called "Sapir-Whorf hypothesis" states that "language functions, not simply as a device for reporting experience, but also, and more significantly, as a way of defining experience for its speakers."[32] That is to say, we cannot conceive of or communicate a reality that has not first been defined for us by our own linguistic apparatus. Private experience and scientific data both depend on and are fashioned by our mental constitution. In a variety of terms, then, aspects of this same problem are now facing physics, neuropsychology, and linguistics: there is no objective world for man to observe and study, for in every field of research he confronts his own reflection.

Among the books that stimulated the creation of "The New Knowledge" the most important single one is Werner Heitler's *Man and Science*, which Sjöstrand read in its first German edition of 1961. Professor of physics in Zürich and known for his contribution to the Heitler-London quantum theory of the chemical bond, Heitler in this book reviews the basic assumptions made in contemporary science and arrives at the conclusion that "there is probably no sharp dividing line, free from any arbitrariness, between an external world . . . and our inner life."[33] Physics has built its well-ordered universe at the cost of all human qualities and values. It has entrenched itself within the barriers of quantitative mathematical analysis, refusing to let in anything that cannot be subjected to such analysis. "The sole purpose of this book," Heitler writes, "has been to push open a door; a door in a barrier that surrounds the region of validity of present-day science."[34] What Heitler has to say concerning the crucial question of the objectivity and independence of the physical laws, deserves quoting at some length here:

Mathematics is not a natural science. Mathematical relations and laws are not material in nature, and are not to be equated to a physical process. At first sight mathematics appears as a pure creation of the human intellect, comparable rather with a work of art. . . . What can this product of our own intellect have to do with the world around us and its laws, with the external world which is said to be completely detached from and independent of man? Looked at in this way it would be a completely incomprehensible miracle if the world should obey laws expressible only by means of the mathematics we have ourselves invented.

Our mental activity and the external physical world cannot be as independent of each other as this. Even classical physics with the complex mathematical laws that govern its course forces us to the conclusion that our intelligence is somehow very intimately bound up with this external world. It is this connection that allows us to recognize these laws at all. We can hardly assume that a planet knows the nature of a geodesic in Riemannian geometry on which it has to move and indeed demonstrably does move. How does it come about that it moves according to such complex and deep mathematical laws? In one way or another the conclusion is inescapable that there also exists outside of us something of the nature of intelligence—some spiritual principle—associated with the laws and events of the material world and with our mental activity. And so we are brought to the borders of metaphysics.[35]

As the translator aptly notes, "spiritual" is but a rough equivalent of the original "geistig" and carries no religious overtones. Heitler is not a mystic, he just pushes the thoughts and intuitions of many contemporary scientists to their inevitable conclusion.

This, then, is the meaning of the scientist's sudden discovery in "The New Knowledge." In the facts of the physical world he discerns the reflection of his own thoughts and "he senses the inner vision's paths / of light, the human hope." Reality, according to Heitler, has a twofold character: the outward character of quantitative science and the inward character of qualitative human experience. Both are equally true and necessary to the complete understanding of man and the universe. If the inward quality is excluded, if science is divorced from human values, it becomes a threat to humanity, as is only too obvious in the age of the Bomb. The hope of man lies in the integration of science and human values. In his moment of sudden insight Sjöstrand's physicist

> discerns
> just when the reflection breaks,
> the vanishing contours
> of himself, of the Helper, the Friend . . .

In his personification of inward reality as a Helper and Friend, Sjöstrand approaches religious scientists like Teilhard de Chardin whose *Phenomenon of Man* made a deep impression on his thought, but even Heitler claims to show "some of the realities that exist and indeed particularly concern us as human beings, but which are outside of what science treats nowadays or even regards as real. They are realities which give us an inkling of scarcely known—perhaps previously surmised and now forgotten—spiritual facts and efficacies. . . ."³⁶ The concept of a transcendent Helper would be outside Heitler's perspective, but among the forgotten insights he does mention the idealistic systems of Pythagoras and Plato.

To Sjöstrand himself, the Helper certainly has a religious meaning, though it is difficult to name the status or species of this deity. Perhaps it is most readily understood in the Indian terms of Atman and Brahman, in which case the Helper and Friend would be that which, in individual man, partakes of the one, common, infinite, divine mind or spirit. Regarding "The New Knowledge" in the general context of the book in which it appears, *In the Sign of Aquarius*, it would seem legitimate also to identify the Helper and Friend with Christ, granting a somewhat heterodox view of the nature and function of Christ to be explained in the final chapter of this book. Leaving the explicitly religious questions open for the moment, however, the present discussion will be restricted to the relationship between poetry and science, which as we have seen can be treated in terms of subjectivity and objectivity.

The whole problem of the subjective and the objective, of mind and matter, may be described as the problem of qualitative experience as against quantitative description and analysis. And the paradigm of this controversy is the nature of colors. Significantly, Sjöstrand's physicist

> leans in over the fleeing galaxies,
> the prism of colors.

The connection between the two objects of his study is no doubt the red "Doppler" shift in the spectrogram of celestial bodies, assumed, on that evidence, to be traveling away from earth, sometimes at fantastic speeds approaching that of light itself. But the "prism of colors" also raises the question of what colors really are. According to Newton and those who developed his more crude conceptions of light, colors are explained by the laws of the refraction of light, *i.e.* they are quantitative properties of mechanical movement. Against this view Goethe waged a passionate war defending the reality of qualitative difference in colors irreducible to quantitative calculation. In a chapter called "Goethe versus Newton," Heitler, while of course granting the validity of optical analysis in Newton's sense, shows that Goethe's criticism, though often mistaken in detail, should not be treated with contempt. Goethe was one of the first to oppose the claims of physics to have explained away qualitative experience as merely subjective, arbitrary, and even illusive. He realized the threat of such physics to human dignity and artistic creativity. If colors are to be explained away, what is left for the poet and painter but an idle game of illusions? Perhaps only the proclamation of art for art's sake, art as an autonomous realm wholly divorced from the world of physical reality. The second alternative has been the choice of many Romantics, Symbolists, and Modernists, but Sjöstrand refuses to withdraw into the ivory tower of absolute art as much as he refuses to succumb to the tyranny of positivistic science. The "new" knowledge is also a knowledge of new possibilities for the liberation of art both from imitative dependence on physical reality and total alienation from that reality.

In fact, a rapprochement between science and art seems to be envisaged by some advanced scientific theorists. To quote an author writing a few years after Sjöstrand completed his poem, the London physicist David Bohm suggests in an essay with the modest title "Further Remarks on Order":

Thus physics deals with properties, such as mass, length, time, change, etc., which are supposed to exist "out there" independently of human beings, while qualities like harmony and conflict, beauty and ugliness, are supposed to exist only in the eye of the beholder.

I regard it as very important to question this division. Actually, the concepts of length, time, mass, change, have been created by man. A few thousand years ago, nobody felt that these qualities are what is "out there." It is true that they are creations that in some way reflect a reality beyond man's thoughts. Nevertheless, man sees them in nature, as he can see beauty and ugliness.[37]

The intimate relationship between science and art in the
"new" knowledge is emphasized by the allusion contained in
the second paragraph of Sjöstrand's poem:

> He thinks that he thinks . . . He thinks
> in the stuff reality and dreams are woven of

The last line is of course a paraphrase of Prospero's famous
words in *The Tempest*, and some lines further on in the poem
a couple of words are echoed from the same speech in Shakespeare's play: "dissolves in air / thin air." Prospero himself can
be seen as a symbol of the unity of science and art—in his magic
the two are fused—and as one of the Faustian figures of the
Renaissance period who wished to penetrate beyond ordinary
knowledge, Prospero is for Sjöstrand a forerunner of or a symbol
for what the modern scientist ought to be. What he has in common with the modern scientist is the power to subjugate the
forces of nature. They ought also to feel in common a sense of
responsibility for exercising this power, and to manifest the will
to discover and liberate not only physical but also spiritual energy.
To put the half-animal Caliban in thrall does not cause Prospero
great difficulty, but to let the proud airy spirit Ariel go free is
his last and most difficult feat.

Both of the *Tempest* quotations come from the speech Prospero addresses to Ferdinand and Miranda after their wedding
feast—a feast celebrated with a mythological masque staged by
Prospero's servant Ariel by means of airy illusions. The play is
now done, the performers have dissolved into nothing and for
Prospero the whole thing becomes an image of all existence:

> be cheerful sir.
> Our revels now are ended. These our actors,
> As I foretold you, were all spirits and
> Are melted into air, into thin air:
> And, like the baseless fabric of this vision,
> The cloud-capped towers, the gorgeous palaces
> The solemn temples, the great globe itself,
> Yea, all which it inherit, shall dissolve,
> And, like this insubstantial pageant faded,

>   Leave not a rack behind. We are such stuff
>   As dreams are made on: and our little life
>   Is rounded with a sleep.

It is the expansive Renaissance man, happy in discovery, hungry for knowledge and with a lust for power who speaks in these lines, but at the same time one of the period's mystical nature philosophers for whom the material world is a fleeting illusion, an appearance which slips out of the scientist's hands the more he attempts to grasp it. In Sjöstrand's interpretation, Prospero also speaks for the modern scientist with his growing insight into the immaterial essence of being. The barrier between matter and mind has broken down, which is underlined by Sjöstrand's amplification of Shakespeare's lines: "of the same stuff as reality and dreams are made of." Dream and reality can no longer be regarded as polar opposites.

In *The Tempest*, the one who conjures up the mythological phantasmagoria is Ariel, the airy spirit, who longs to be freed from his service with Prospero, whom however he loves and venerates. The creative spirit is free and must not be used for destructive purposes. Ariel is a helper who lives on the border between spirit and nature. For Sjöstrand's modern Prospero, in "The New Knowledge," Ariel's form has to some degree been changed, but many of the original features remain—the airy essence, the invisible voice:

>   Like a violent swirl
>   through his generation's thoughts and formulae
>   (for the simple and the difficult) he hears
>   the voice he has almost forgotten and denied—

The occurrence of the allusion to *The Tempest* immediately after the lines inspired by Heitler's ideas suggests a close connection, in Sjöstrand's mind, between those ideas and Shakespeare's play. What they have in common is the general doubt as to the solidity of matter and temporal existence and the belief in something behind the world of appearance. Perhaps they also have a common source. As was mentioned, Heitler names Pythagoras and Plato among those ancient nature philosophers who seem to have divined the answers to some of the fundamental questions puzzling present-day physicists.[38] And the critical hypothesis that the ideas of *The Tempest* derive from ancient Platonism and mystery religion, has certainly not been lost on Sjöstrand who is a keen student of the history of Platonism. The fact that similar ideas were current during the Renaissance and in our own time, with a period of rigid scientific dogmatism in between, is a further point of great interest to Sjöstrand—to be explained in connection with his views on history in the concluding chapter of this book.[39]

A final point of analogy between Prospero and the present-day scientist is the question of responsibility. It lies within Prospero's power to use his magic for both good and evil and the play clearly demonstrates that without moral responsibility knowledge may be disastrous. The contemporary version of this dilemma is only too well known. Man's abuse of the power he has obtained over nature is a recurrent theme in Sjöstrand's recent poetry, and this abuse is linked with the attitude to the power man has succeeded in liberating. In "liberating" thermonuclear energy scientists seem to have penetrated into the very secret of matter which reveals itself as energy or perhaps something even more spiritual. In a searching question as to the inner continuity of the material world, Sjöstrand uses the word "will":

> A conductive matter? An unbroken will, from uranium to
>   lead, in heat and acid?
> —For the rapacious, the greedy of gain: roof-beams that
>   will break, the stone
> thrown against themselves . . . For all the unselfish,
>   unafraid spirits (on the sea that She beheld):
> The Sign which prompted them forward[40]

The person who utters those words is Wisdom, personified as a kind of genius or goddess, and by the rapacious and greedy she surely has in view the politicians, the military and technical men who in their exploiting of atomic power run the risk of being struck by their own weapons, of blowing their houses into air, and destroying the earth they inhabit. But for the unselfish and the intrepid, for the humbly inquiring spirit, the liberated power becomes a prompting for wider investigation and deeper insight. Man must look at his own reflection in the universe with unselfish eyes in order to discern what "The New Knowledge" calls the Helper, the Friend.

It is obvious, then, that the "new" knowledge is something more than a new scientific theory. It is rather the fusion of creative imagination with scientific investigation, of the two cultures in a new whole. And the language of this fusion is poetry. In this commentary on "The New Knowledge," attention has mainly been given to the underlying ideas because it seemed to be there that commentary was most needed. But it is of course only in their poetic context that the ideas become emotionally effective. The protagonist is no mere typification of the modern scientist, he is set against a background of professional and everyday circumstances. He is not an isolated mind but a human being and a member of human society, not only a dreaming philosopher but a worker—as an astronomer sharing the routine of any night-shift worker. The "new" knowledge, Sjöstrand seems to say, is not an abstraction, not an intellectual system, but a new way of life changing ordinary people from within.

V *The Hidden Music*

Mathematics and poetry as symbolic representations of experience are generally regarded as being at opposite ends of the gamut of verbal communication. In mathematics the verbal element is of course reduced to figures, algebraic symbols, signs of operation, etc., whereas in poetry the words are treated in the opposite way: instead of being depleted of their concrete sensuous meaning, they receive, as it were, an extra charge of meaning by the addition of subtle, intense emotional qualities. And in between lies the broad register of ordinary common-sense language into which mathematics can, in principle, be amplified, and in which poetry can be paraphrased in a crude way and at the loss of that extra charge. This conception of the status of poetry in relation to mathematics is no doubt useful for many critical purposes, but it obscures important similarities between poetry and mathematics as symbolic, shorthand versions of ordinary language.

The usefulness of mathematics lies in its enabling us to handle complex relations between vast quantities of data. Correspondingly, the usefulness of poetry lies in its enabling us to handle complex relations between different qualities of experience. In both cases it is a matter of extending the compass of the mind, of making it possible to present to the mind's eye a complex yet clearly structured picture which it would take too long to describe in ordinary language—too long for the mind to grasp it as a whole. The fact that mathematics is concerned with relating quantities to each other and poetry with qualities makes no difference in this respect. It is the shorthand technique for handling complex relationships they have in common.

Proposing this analogy between a mathematical formula and a poem entails no claims to have defined or exhausted the meaning of poetic language. However, it may perhaps shed some light on the way whole systems of ideas are sometimes integrated in a poem without explicit references. A single word or image may serve as a pointer signaling the reader to actualize his knowledge of a whole sphere of ideas. As this knowledge is brought to mind, it is adapted to the intellectual and emotional structure laid down by the poem. The same of course applies to other kinds of experience than ideas; it is indeed the normal case that the "formula" of a poem controls sets of predominantly emotional rather than intellectual qualities. But since Sjöstrand's scientifically inspired poetry depends so much on ideas, it seems justified here to dwell specifically on the integration of complicated intellectual material in poetry. "The New Knowledge," already discussed, revealed a variety of barely hinted-at ideas and scientific concepts unified by the comprehensive "formula" of the poem. "The Hidden Music," now to be discussed, contains within its 33 lines an even wider variety of ideas and conceptions held together by an even more precise "formula." In passing it may be mentioned that the number 33 is not without significance in the history of poetry. At its root lies the holy trinity, and 33 is the number of cantos in each division of Dante's *Divina Commedia*. And since Sjöstrand deliberately decided on 33 lines, that would serve to hint at the scope of his intentions in "The Hidden Music," which is, in its kind, a cosmography.

Before leaving the topic of poetry and mathematics a third term must be introduced into the equation, music. The affinity between music and mathematics is obvious—up to the Renaissance music was indeed considered a branch of mathematics. And the musical aspects of poetry have been discussed at length in this book. Reverting to the popular view of mathematics and poetry as located at opposite ends of the gamut of language, music could, by way of a fanciful metaphor, be likened to the span of an arch soaring from one end to the other high up in the ether of pure emotional forms above the groundling language of ordinary words. That is to say, insofar as poetry contains an element of music, it also partakes of the essence of mathematics, and a recognition of this possibility helps us to establish the frame of mind needed to understand and appreciate Sjöstrand's synthesis of, among other things, Indian philosophy, Pythagorean theory of music, the astronomy of Kepler, and modern geometrodynamics. The formula sounds forbidding, but the poem that grew out of it has a sensuous simplicity unrivaled in Sjöstrand's work.

The Hidden Music

"Be cheerful, sir, our revels now are ended"

I

Time of the earth crust.
Time of the galactic star clusters.
Time of the wagtail.

Once:
an oceanic movement,
a wave to imitate.

Now: the countless
sunlit dust specks trembling
in each opening window.

In the rose window of equations.
In the cathedral of mathematics—

          a world which still lives
with us, with the mind and senses of man,
          with men who measure—
          who discover new, fleeing
          star clusters beyond the horizon
          and reach out towards echoes

of voices, beyond the sea ice and the ground frost
          and sleepless nights
in cities, where the ground water dries—

          voices we loved, love—

          Patiently, tirelessly,
          we seek to free matter itself,
          the frozen spirit.

          Some time: time of man . . .

               II

          While shining night clouds,
          dark nebulae, draw past,
          I listen—not

to the sunk cathedral's bells
          which fall silent
          with the distant ocean.

          I hear a pulsing universe
          inside my closed eyelids.[41]

The motto from the same speech of Prospero's that Sjöstrand alludes to in "The New Knowledge" suggests that the two poems are concerned with the same fundamental issue of appearance and reality, but there are no further references to *The Tempest* in "The Hidden Music." The kind of ideas involved in that poem Sjöstrand briefly indicates in his essay on music and poetry:

By the hidden music I do not in the first place refer to the chiming bells of the engulfed cathedral. . . . What I refer to is the elusive intuition of a "harmonia mundi," a "music of the spheres" in a pulsing universe, in the architecture of matter. This musical infrastructure also has to do with cathedrals past and present, those which in our day are built by mathematicians and scientists. . . . The poem was prompted by some pages in a book on geometrodynamics by the physicist John Archibald Wheeler, professor at Princeton university.[42]

It must be admitted at once that the topic of geometrodynamics is perhaps the most forbidding of all in the whole sphere of physical science, tantalizing the common reader with its mathematical abstractions appearing to dissolve in the thin air of nothingness, yet at the same time holding out promises of explaining the very basis of physical existence. Wheeler's own definition of his subject in the second sentence of the Foreword to his book does away with all expectations of common-sense comprehensibility: "Geometrodynamics is the study of the geometry of curved *empty* space and the evolution of this geometry with time according to the equations of Einstein's standard 1916 general relativity."[43] Any attempt at paraphrase in ordinary words leads to paradox. To the imagination, empty space can be nothing but nothingness, yet Wheeler submits that both matter and energy are best explained as functions of the curvature, indeed as this very curvature, of nothingness. One could rewrite the opening of *Genesis* thus to fit his conceptions: "In the beginning God created empty space. And the empty space was without form, and void; and darkness was upon the face of the deep. And the Spirit of God moved upon the face of the ocean of space. And God said, Let there be time: and there was time. And with time, empty space began to curve, and brought forth worlds without end."

Of course Wheeler does not use God's name. He is not concerned with the question of how it all began. But a more compelling statement than his of creation out of nothing can hardly be imagined. And as we shall presently see, the biblical symbol of formless primordial waters recurs in his explication of geometrodynamics. The whole drama of physical existence is, to his mind, "curved empty space going through its dynamical evolution with time."[44] And on the very pages that seem to have caught Sjöstrand's attention, he lists the paradoxical achievements of his branch of science in language which could be that of a mystic trying to describe the unfathomable mystery of the transcendent Lord of the Creation. Wheeler claims that "geo-metrodynamics—and geometrodynamics alone—has been found to explain not only

> gravitation without gravitation and
> equations of motion without equations of motion, but also mass without mass,
> electromagnetism without electromagnetism,
> coupling constant without coupling constant, and
> charge without charge."[45]

The rapprochement of poetry and science seems to work both ways. For who would deny that Wheeler, though it did not form part of his intention, has here written a poem, or a sketch for a liturgy of science?

So much for Wheeler's general vision—if such a term be permitted of a work that largely consists of mathematical deductions. In order to understand its relevance to Sjöstrand's poem we have to consider one of the metaphors not seldom used by scientists attempting to give a more popular notion of what their equations are about. "The Hidden Music" opens with an invocation of three different temporal phases of the cosmic evolution: "Time of the earth crust. / Time of the galactic star clusters. / Time of the wagtail"—*i.e.* geological time, astronomical time, and biological time. But before those

> Once:
> an oceanic movement,
> a wave to imitate.

Here we are brought back to the very beginning when empty space first began to curve. In his commentary Sjöstrand mentions that primordial space is known to scientists under many names, among them that of "Dirac's ocean" (after the British physicist Paul Dirac), and Wheeler adopts the same metaphor:

Is it reasonable to compare the singularities which arise in the geometry in the recontraction phase of a closed universe with the curling crests and cusps which develop on an ocean wave as it moves into shallow water? In the hydrodynamic case a limit is set to the sharpness of any incipient singularities by the action of capillarity. The lengthening and thinning sheet of water at the overturning crest is broken up into droplets and foam by surface tension. Is there a similar effective limit set to the sharpness of the curvature of space-time by the quantum of action?[46]

It was the metaphor of the ocean of space-time as such that stirred Sjöstrand's imagination but he also quotes Wheeler's estimate of the average dimension of the droplets or eddies of the ocean of space, $1,6 \cdot 10^{-33}$ cm.[47]

Now, to Sjöstrand waves and oceans are, as we have seen, always associated with music. Which would in this case result in the orientation:

$$\text{space-time} = \text{ocean} = \text{music}$$

This orientation can be regarded as the successive links in a chain of metaphoric associations, but it is more than that. In Sjöstrand's interpretation it implies a set of structural analogies. And if the middle term is left out for the moment and space-time and music are considered together, we confront the old Pythagorean conception of the "music of the spheres," which Kepler developed into his fantastic though exact formulas for the harmonic relations between the various planetary orbits. His general idea was, as is well known, that the same arithmetical symmetries apply to both musical harmonics and celestial mechanics; if the revolution of the heavenly spheres could be heard by human ears, that would be the most perfect harmony ever heard, because it is the most perfect harmony conceivable.

When Sjöstrand in his commentary speaks of a "harmonia mundi," it is of course Kepler that first springs to mind, but in fact it was a modern writer who gave his thoughts that direction at the time of conceiving "The Hidden Music," Paul Hindemith in his book, A Composer's World. Horizons and Limitations.[48] Speaking of that "musica mundana" which controls the orbits of planets and holds together the universe in one effective harmony, Hindemith recalls the uniting by the ancients of music, geometry, arithmetic, and astronomy into the so-called quadrivium, which together constituted the arts of measurement and topological analysis. Music as one of the scientific researcher's tools or modes of analysis is no baffling conception to Hindemith, who foresees a possible convergence in the future of music and the exact sciences.

Against the triplet dealing with the "oceanic movement" of empty space, Sjöstrand poses a contrasting triplet. Once, that movement only,

> Now: the countless
> sunlit dust specks trembling
> in each opening window.

This self-contained visual image, calling attention to the ceaseless movement of minute particles in our immediate surroundings, opens up wide philosophical perspectives if we follow Sjöstrand's hints in his commentary. The image, he tells us, was prompted by some lines from the *Bhagavata-Purana* which he happened to have studied only a few months before he came across Wheeler's book:

> Like sunlit dust specks
> streaming through open windows,
> through Mahavishnu's pores
> countless universes stream.
> As He exhales they come to be,
> as He inhales they perish.
> This cycle never ends,
> for ever worlds are born and die,
> for ever Mahavishnu breathes.[49]

It has proved impossible exactly to locate these lines—European translations of the *Bhagavata-Purana* vary to a baffling extent and Sjöstrand has forgotten which one he used, perhaps an English translation, perhaps a German one. However, the essential idea of the quotation is easy to find, expressed in various ways in different contexts. Compare for instance the following passage from Swami Prabhavananda's version of the *Purana*:

Creation, O Vidura, has no absolute beginning. The present universe is but one of a series of worlds that are past and of worlds that are

to be. The cosmic energy alternates between periods of potentiality
and of expression. The phase of potentiality is known as dissolution;
the phase of expression is known as creation.[50]

The coupling of this creative pulse with breathing, as in the
lines about Mahavishnu, is natural in view of the importance
attached to breathing by Indian philosophers and yogi alike. In
the words of the *Taittriya Upanishad*:

> The gods do breathe along with breath,
> As also men and beasts.
> For truly, breath is the life of beings.
> Therefore it is called the Life-of-all.[51]

The connection between breathing and music is obvious: the
lines of melody, the accents of phrasing, the pulse of rhythm
are all, in one aspect, structures superimposed upon the natural
time of inhalation and exhalation. So it is fully consistent with
the conception of a musical "harmonia mundi" to imagine the creative, and destructive, force as the breath of the Creator himself.

The *Taittriya Upanishad*, or rather Sankaracharya's commentary to it, also belongs to the field of reference of "The
Hidden Music." As Sjöstrand points out, Wheeler is a scientist
of wide perspectives, and among those who have foreshadowed
modern geometrodynamics he mentions the sixteenth-century
Italian writer F. Patrizzi, and after quoting him, Wheeler adds:
"Also some of the Vedas of old India suggest that the idea is
very old, that nature derives its whole structure and way of
action from properties of space. Can space be regarded as a mar-
vellous creation of all-encompassing properties? Independent of
the origins of this idea, both ancient and modern, let us now proceed to analyze it. . . ."[52] And in a long footnote Wheeler quotes
Sankaracharya and other commentators on the *Upanishads* ex-
pounding the concept of "akasa," or space. And Sjöstrand's com-
ment to these pages in Wheeler is emphatic: "This juxtaposition
of the modern scientific view of the world and Indian philosophy
came largely to direct the shaping of the poem. . . ."[53]

A further point of connection between "The Hidden Music"

and ancient Indian thought can merely be indicated here. In his commentary Sjöstrand mentions that in the first three lines of the poem he has "tried to adopt three of the Hindu rhythms, deshi-talas. The connection is not as fortuitous as it may first seem. As is well known, the Indian view of these rhythms merges into the view of the cosmic totality...."[54] An attempt to demonstrate what Sjöstrand claims to have done by way of rhythmic arrangements in the opening lines must of course be restricted to the Swedish original and cannot be undertaken here. However, a few words by the expert on Indian music, Arnold Bake, may serve to support and amplify Sjöstrand's statement. On the role of music in ancient Hindu liturgy, Bake writes: "The correctly recited word or the correctly sung note were the carriers of cosmic creativity. The idea of musical sound as the archetypal principle of creation, fully elaborated in the later philosophy, is to be found already in Vedic times."[55] Thus the poet joins the scientist in the task of freeing the "frozen spirit," the "hidden music."

Having indicated the sources and ideas in "The Hidden Music," we can revert to the problem of how these various sources and ideas are brought together in the unifying "formula" of the poem. Guided by modern physics and ancient Indian philosophy, the poet arrives at the intuition of a primordial substance underlying all reality, prior to matter and energy, manifesting itself in the dynamic temporal evolution of the universe, from the composition of nebulae, stars, and galaxies up to the emergence of life and mind. In one of its aspects this evolution is comparable to music, *is* music. The musical structuring of the primordial substance lies embedded in the physical appearance of reality, it is a "hidden" music to be discovered and liberated by the inquiring, creative mind of man. As the anonymous medieval master-builders erected their cathedrals in the image of and to the glory of God, the Builder of the Universe, so modern mathematicians erect the proud structure of science—in the image of and to the glory of the mind of man.

> In the rose window of equations.
> In the cathedral of mathematics.

The poem goes on to affirm that in these vast, abstract structures of mathematical science is contained "a world which still lives / with us, with the mind and senses of man." A world in which man not only carries on his indefatigable research but strives to establish contact and communication with his fellowmen; a world where men "reach out towards echoes / of . . . voices we loved, love." The emotional relationship between men and the mathematical relationship between physical elements are both structures emerging in the course of cosmic evolution, are both permeated by the "hidden music" that lies at the root of all existence. And the direction of cosmic evolution is toward increasing consciousness of itself and of its own music:

> Patiently, tirelessly,
> we seek to free matter itself,
> the frozen spirit.
> Some time: time of man . . .

The "some time" corresponds to the "once" and "now" in lines four and seven, and hints at a coming age of spiritual fulfillment, the age of the "new knowledge."

The shorter second part of the poem has the character of a personal afterthought. After the objective statements in the third person of the earlier part the poet speaks in the first person—"I listen," "I hear." While the cosmic appearances draw past his vision, he directs his hearing to the hidden music, but not the music of the Engulfed Cathedral, of obliterated doctrines and beliefs of the past, his own past. He discovers the rhythm of the music within himself:

> I hear a pulsing universe
> inside my closed eyelids.

In a note to these lines Sjöstrand emphasizes the word "inside": "it is thus not a question of taking sides in the cosmological debate,"[56] i.e. the debate whether the history of the universe is an oscillation between successive states of cosmic expansion and contraction, or a less dramatic affair of a steady state. Fred Hoyle, one of the authors of the steady-state theory, published a popular book on this subject in 1966, which appeared in Swedish translation that same year.[57]

The "pulsing universe" which the speaker in "The Hidden Music" hears inside himself is a pulse of infinitesimal frequency compared with that of the cosmological eons; it is the pulse of existence emerging out of the primordial ocean of empty space. Through the rhythms of his biological functions, including the unfathomably complex but likewise rhythmical workings of the nervous system, man is immediately connected with the "harmonia mundi." And it is the task of the poet to free these rhythms, to transform them into self-contained works of art which in turn may act as liberators of the music hidden within the readers.

CHAPTER 4

Poetry and the Future

I Toward a Poetry of the Future

THE feeling that we are living in an era of transition seems to have been gathering strength as the twentieth century has proceeded from its optimistic beginnings during "La Belle Epoque," through a series of wars and political crises up to the present situation of general social unrest fanned by threats of disaster and annihilation through nuclear warfare, population explosion, and pollution of the entire human environment. Such threats, each apparently leading to catastrophe, also seem to develop at accelerating speed, and whether optimists or pessimists most people seem inclined to agree that drastic changes in our way of occupying and using the earth are imminent. In literature this situation is most obviously reflected in science fiction, but recently it has begun to affect poetry as well. And Östen Sjöstrand was one of the first, not only in Sweden, to have accepted such a concern as a vital part of the poet's function.

The present situation dates, of course, from the first atomic bomb in 1945, but the foundations of the "old world" were heavily rocked by the First World War, and one of the first poetic expressions of this feeling to win general recognition was *The Waste Land*. With the irony typical of that poem, T. S. Eliot chose a bartender's trivial cry at closing time as a presentiment of the approaching spiritual night: "HURRY UP PLEASE ITS TIME." To Eliot, writing a few years after the First World War, the material destruction of the foundations of life on earth was still an unknown threat. It was the social, cultural, and spiritual disintegration of postwar Europe that concerned him, but the feeling of imminent danger cannot be mistaken. A couple of years after

The Waste Land he foresaw the end of the world "Not with a bang but a whimper."[1]

Doomsday notes were sounded in Swedish poetry, too, at about the same time. Living in Germany at the end of the First World War Bertil Malmberg composed his "Song to the World's Darkness," invoking the four apocalyptic horses of the Book of Revelation. And some fifteen years later, when German National Socialism began to show its true and threatening face, he wrote the poem "Midnight," fearfully celebrating a world "in the grip of an unspeakable enchantment," plunging into the depths of archaic barbarity.[2] The book inaugurating lyric modernism in Sweden belongs to the same apocalyptic sphere. It is Gunnar Ekelöf's *Late on Earth* (1932), technically inspired by the dreamlike disintegration of reality practiced by the French Surrealists. With uncanny foresight he proclaimed that "tomorrow the atom will be split,"[3] and the feeling of approaching catastrophe pervades the whole book.

A question highly relevant to the study of those three poets and to the many others writing in the same vein, including Sjöstrand in his apocalyptic mood, is to what extent their feelings of impending disaster are merely projections of their private inner conflicts. It is a well-known fact that Eliot wrote *The Waste Land* convalescing after a nervous breakdown and that he was much surprised to learn, on its publication, that he had given voice to the despair of a whole generation.[4] In Malmberg's case the personal background of the first poem mentioned was one of guilt-ridden depression following upon wild dissipations in the bohemian circles of Munich,[5] and Ekelöf's state of mind at the time of writing *Late on Earth* was, owing to grave emotional disturbances, frankly suicidal.[6] Of Sjöstrand's recurrent depressions and guilt-haunted conscience enough has been said earlier in this book. All four were sufficiently enlightened, psychiatrically speaking, to realize the error of confusing personal despair with a real threat to the existing world order, at least when they had distanced themselves from the dark mood far enough to transform it into poetry.

But the question is not as easy as that. To explain away apocalyptic poetry by reference to the author's state of mental health would be the cheapest form of critical psychologizing. One would rather accept the Romantic and Symbolist doctrine of the poet as one suffering vicariously for all mankind and prophetically foreseeing evils to come, though perhaps not by means of some sort of divine inspiration but by that deliberate disorder of the senses of which Rimbaud writes in a famous letter: "Je dis qu'il faut être *voyant*, se faire *voyant*. Le Poète se fait *voyant* par un long, immense et raisonné *dérèglement* de *tous les sens*."[7] It is far from clear what kind of "seeing" Rimbaud had in mind; that it has prophetic overtones follows from his words at the beginning of the same letter about "l'avenir de la poésie," the future of poetry. And as to the "raisonné dérèglement," Sjöstrand's words, "I am a pharmacist—I transform poisons into remedies...,"[8] amount to the same. The emotional and mental disturbance of so many poets must not be taken as the cause of their art in the sense that it explains away the objective meaning and the message, but rather as a condition necessary to deeper insights. What they see may be real and objective enough, however great the amount of personal illness and suffering involved.

Granting the claim of the apocalyptic poets that their visions and warnings refer to realities outside their personal states of mind, we have to counter another interpretation which would minimize the extent to which those poets could foresee disasters or revolutions in the objective dimension of historical evolution. Their visions may not be restricted to their private minds but may nevertheless be confined within the boundaries of psychology, *i.e.* the common mind of the age, or even of all ages. The psychoanalysis developed by C. G. Jung and his followers emphasizes universal characteristics; they claim to discover again and again the same deeply significant emotional patterns and images in the dreams and intuitive creations of men and women from widely separate times, regions, and societies. Among these archetypes, as they call them, are also images of destruction, death and rebirth, expressive of eternally reenacted dramas of the soul which are given objective form in myth, ritual, and art. These archetypal patterns and images are essentially timeless, it is only when objectified in myth and art that they take on a temporal, historical dimension, which, however, is secondary.[9]

The prophets of the Old Testament, the Book of Revelation, the art of for instance William Blake—they have all been explained in this way.

This is not a mode of interpretation invented by modern depth psychology. We find it in many mystic writings. Meister Eckhart, for instance, to whom Sjöstrand has devoted much study, speaks in a sermon of the kingdom of heaven not as a realm beyond or in the future but as a state of being eternally present to those who have eyes to see it.[10] Whether psychoanalytical or mystic, this mode of interpreting religious and poetic texts inevitably implies doubts as to the reality, or validity, of the dimension of time and history, and in studying a poet like Sjöstrand with his leanings toward both psychoanalysis and mysticism, these doubts must always occur to the reader.

However, not even the saints and mystics dwell permanently in the kingdom of heaven, nor the poets in the archetypal realm of the unconscious soul. Time and history are real enough, and just as in theology mysticism is counterbalanced by eschatology, so the timeless psychological patterns in twentieth-century poetry are counterbalanced by a deep concern with the course of history. The era of depth psychology is also the era of dialectical historicism, to mention only one modern school in the philosophy of history.

The dialectical view of history in the tradition of Hegel and Marx tends, of course, to develop into utopianism, absorbing as it has much of the late nineteenth-century evolutionary optimism. This kind of optimism is, however, absent from most of the original poetry written after the First World War. Revolutionary dreams are not lacking, but more typical of the interwar age is the bitter disappointment voiced by writers who at some stage in their career put their faith in Communism. As the Second World War approached, pessimism and evil forebodings spread all over Europe, not least in Sweden, and the fact that Sweden was spared from invasion when the rest of Scandinavia was occupied by the Germans early in the war, brought little relief to the gloom of the nation. In the early 1940's there was a brief outburst of patriotism among Swedish poets who sought release from their fears and fulfillment of their vague hopes in the limited perspective of political freedom and national integrity; but their apocalyptic imagery was mainly rhetoric.[11]

More detached from the short-term political developments, some philosophers of history of the interwar period elaborated periodic systems of history according to which the twentieth century is a crucial turning-point. Most influential was Oswald Spengler's *The Decline of the West* (1918–1922), according to which Western civilization and Christianity had run their course, leaving the contemporary world in the turmoil of transition toward an unknown and uncertain future. Disagreeing with Spengler's fatalism, Arnold Toynbee also claimed to discover periodic patterns in the evolution of history. Earlier than these historians similar ideas were put to poetic use by W. B. Yeats. In his strange mixture of occult tradition and private revelation, the conception of a "new dawn," of a spiritual, cultural, and political rebirth becomes prominent in the late 1910's and permeates his later work, *e.g.* the poem "The Second Coming" and the fantastic prose treatise *A Vision*. Those who could not share Yeats's faith in the dawn of a new era could at least recognize his feeling of the decline of old values and the pains of living through a period of transition without direction. An older conception of the periodic system of history, propounded by Vico in the eighteenth century, was utilized in the equally esoteric but more influential writings of James Joyce.

An important contribution to the twentieth-century philosophy of history came from Friedrich Nietzsche, a powerful influence on both German and Swedish poetry up to the Second World War. His twin ideas of the coming of superman and of eternal recurrence combined to foster a belief in a new golden age to come when mankind would have rid itself of its Christian inhibitions and petty bourgeois morality. In Germany Nietzsche's prophet Stefan George formed a group of disciples to whom he dedicated his poetry proclaiming the advent of the new Reich, the kingdom of the chosen few who were to govern the world. In Finland the works of Nietzsche came as a revelation to the poetess Edith Södergran, who living within hearing of the guns at the Russian frontier during the First World War triumphantly announced that "The world is bathing in blood that God may live"—a deity very different from the Christian God but close to the "Genius of the Apocalypse" whom she celebrated in another poem at that time.[12] These were extravagancies unique in contemporary Swedish-language poetry, but Edith Södergran's general influence on the following generations of poets was great.

Those who thought the war would inaugurate a new and happy era were as disappointed as those who had perhaps hoped that the old world would survive. The 1920's are notorious for their disillusionment and cynicism. But the Nietzschean heritage was not spent. Twisted and vulgarized, it entered into the doctrine of German National Socialism which also seized upon the visions of Stefan George, ignoring that both he and Nietzsche had been prophets of a spiritual kingdom and had heartily despised politics and militarism. So it came about that in Germany some of the loftiest and most idealistic visions of man's future were abused and transformed into that all too well-known gospel of the golden age of Aryan reign over the world. Culturally under German dominion for more than a century, Sweden was deplorably susceptible to this gospel, dazzled by the spectacular recovery of German society during the 1930's and unable to believe that the long-established and much imitated rhetoric of German Idealism had suddenly been put to such infernal uses.

The clash between the pro- and anti-German political camps in Sweden during the Second World War was experienced at first-hand by the young Sjöstrand, who enjoyed the military exercises, the comradeship and the social activities in the conservative youth movement while at school; and in the leading Gothenburg newspaper he daily confronted a staunch liberal opposition against everything German. The outcome of the war and the revelation of the atrocities committed in the concentration camps cured him permanently of all trust in utopias based on racial distinctions and military power.

The postwar years hardly invited hopes of a new golden age. Insofar as a decisive turning-point in history was envisaged, it was for the worse: total annihilation through nuclear warfare. It is symptomatic that the fiction and poetry of the late 1940's in Sweden turned its back on the idea of progress and historical evolution and concentrated on the timeless aspects of the human

condition. Kafka and French Existentialism were among the chief
foreign influences and anxiety was a dominant literary theme.
These were also the years of a violent controversy over the claims
of Christianity, carried on in newspapers and public lectures
and debates and attracting a great number of prominent writers.
While Christianity was publicly denounced as dishonest supersti-
tion and the Lutheran theologians and bishops kept up a pathetic
defense, in this situation Roman Catholicism insinuated itself
into the minds of a small minority of intellectuals, and as we
have already seen in Chapter 1, Sjöstrand was one of those who
took refuge in the Church from disappointment with the world
and from personal anxiety. And within the Church he was drawn
toward the most unworldly theology and mysticism, wishing to
renounce all part in temporal affairs—wishing, in fact, to withdraw from history.

But that withdrawal, as we have seen, was a foredoomed act
of desperation. When during the 1950's Sjöstrand gradually
emerged from his isolation as a man and a poet and allowed himself to get involved in temporal matters, that was in itself a line
of development he had in common with the majority of young
writers in Sweden. Yet he appeared as an outsider, largely because of his outward allegiance to the Roman Catholic faith,
and also because he could not share the commitment to political
radicalism which served as an avenue of escape from personal
anxiety to many poets and novelists, especially in the 1960's. He
could not bring himself to believe that theirs was a realistic, or
even a desirable solution to the problems of the world.

Meanwhile, the scope and gravity of these problems became
increasingly clear to him. Being something of an outsider with
small personal wants, he was little impressed by the sensational
economic growth of the 1950's and 1960's. Living at that time in
an apartment in a typical suburb of Stockholm, he suffered from
the sterility and unfriendly anonymity of modern metropolitan
life, cut off from the natural surroundings that had meant so much
to him ever since childhood. In the habit of reading scientific
journals such as *Nature* and *Scientific American*, he was startled
by the earliest warnings of increased radioactivity in the atmosphere, of chemical poisoning of air, water, and soil, of ac-

celerating population growth and ruthless exploitation of the natural resources of the earth, of the extinction of whole species of animals and plants, of the deluge of drugs and narcotics by which modern society vainly tries to wash away its anxiety and fears. The whole environmental complex was a personal concern to him years before it became a topical issue.

The question of environment is also a question of the future, and so Sjöstrand was led on to a study of futurology, that new science which, in many respects, may be called a pseudoscience; how could it be anything else? Nevertheless we cannot do without it. We desperately need some frame of reference which will enable us to relate the present to the future. Works like Herman Kahn and Anthony J. Wiener's *The Year 2000. A Framework for Speculation on the Next Thirty-Three Years* (1967) immediately attracted his attention, and he is also a keen student of the German *Zukunftsforschung.* As an academic discipline futurology is concerned with technological, economic, political, and sociological trends and forecasts, and as a branch of the general positivistic social sciences of the West it admits of no spiritual forces in the process of historical evolution. And that is where Sjöstrand parts company with the established science of futurology. Religious at the very roots of his being, he instinctively senses a pattern in history made up of more fundamental elements than economics and technology, and even after his leaving the Roman Catholic Church the general terms of Christian eschatology have remained valid to him.

Sjöstrand's approach to the study of the future, therefore, is nearer in spirit to the speculative systems of history mentioned above than to the present-day futurology. But his "system"—which is not really a systematic body of thought—is a construction put upon the facts and forecasts presented by futurologists. This concern with the topical problems of our time might easily entail a risk of the poetry deteriorating into journalism, but Sjöstrand's work is, I believe, saved from this by the author's early, deep, and very personal relationship to the very elements which are now at stake: as we have seen, air and water are the recurrent themes throughout his poetic work, in which they form not topical ornaments but an integrated symbolism. It is perhaps by bringing this deeply personal concern with the elements to bear on mankind's common predicament in our time that Sjöstrand has made his most original and important contribution to poetry. The purpose of the remaining pages of this book is to show how this concern combines with what was earlier described as the "New Knowledge" into a vision of man's only hope of a future on earth.

First, however, some examples of less complex poems revealing his awakening to the environmental threats.

II   *Earth the Home of Man*

Homelessness and Home, the title of Sjöstrand's 1958 collection, points to the author's double attitude toward life on earth. As part of creation and biological evolution man is a native of the earth which is his true home; but spiritual man "cometh from afar" and is but a guest on earth and his stay is always beset with a feeling of homelessness. This is of course but another version of the old Platonic and Christian view of man's double role as both an eternal and a temporal being, though without the contempt of earthly existence which so often discolors Platonic idealism. A fine example of Sjöstrand's affirmation of the natural life is "In Praise of Deciduous Trees" in *Homelessness and Home,* a poem deeply rooted in the Swedish soil and perhaps not fully at home in any language but Swedish:

> Your choice between oak and spruce
> broad leaf and thin needle
> between trust and loneliness
>
> is the arbiter of Swedish solitude:
> verdure thinned-out is a soul
> thinned-out or darkening in melancholy.
>
> What you gain, your kin lose again . . .
>
> Let the grove keep its fleeting shadow
> the open woodland its secret life
> Let the brook not fall silent under moss
>
> More than the puritan's dream of summer, the leafy meadow
> is the most splendid garden in wild flourishing:
> leafy trees like wine gladden the hearts of men

Eastwood and Southwood and great meadow of Westerplain . . .

Whoever was homeless, even,
or came from another land
heard among the foliage a word of home[13]

The choice between oak and spruce reflects the two types of
Swedish woodland, the proportions of which have been drasti-
cally altered in recent years. The rich forests of oak, beech, birch,
elm, linden, and other deciduous trees that once covered most
of Europe have retained their hold longer in Sweden than on the
continent, though the verdure, owing to climate and soil, never
was so thick and lush there. And the farther north, the more
spruce, pine, and fir become dominant. For hundreds, perhaps
thousands of years, a harmonious equilibrium has been maintained between leaf and needle, between natural woodland and
cultured soil, and in between the two has flourished that typically
Swedish landscape, the leafy meadow, which is the outcome of
pasturing cattle in meager woodland interspersed with meadows
full of wild flowers. The leafy meadow has the appearance of
an uncultured landscape in which nature itself seems to have
created a humble and what Sjöstrand calls a "most splendid
garden in wild flourishing."

Since the Second World War the Swedish countryside has
undergone far-reaching changes. Hundreds of small farms have
closed down each year. Fields and meadows, for innumerable
generations laboriously maintained against encroaching shrubbery
and wood, have been planted with spruce. Growing faster than
deciduous trees and thus yielding higher profit, spruce is increasingly being introduced into the age-old leafy forests as well.
And soil once given over to spruce takes centuries to reclaim for
deciduous vegetation. The choice between spruce and oak is
therefore synonymous with the choice between profit-oriented
technical development and ecologically responsible growth, between short-sighted exploitation of the environment and a consideration for natural and human values in a wider perspective
of past and future.

"In Praise of Deciduous Trees" is one of the very first pleas
in poetic form for the saving of indispensable natural resources
and values, represented and symbolized by the leafy meadow. In

his celebration of that humble landscape Sjöstrand also takes up an old tradition in Swedish literature, once colored by Montesquieu's ideas on the influence of landscape and climate on national character and most influentially expressed by the early nineteenth-century writer C. J. L. Almqvist in his treatise *The Significance of Swedish Poverty*. But to Sjöstrand personally, the meager leafy meadow is "more than the puritan's dream of summer," though the puritan streak in his character is strong. It is the epitome of all that is splendid and lovable in his native environment, it is home for the homeless soul transplanted from its natural surroundings to the sterility of modern metropolitan life.

In the years immediately following *Homelessness and Home*, the threat to the environment became more menacing. The newspapers were full of alarming reports about increased radioactivity in the atmosphere as a result of nuclear tests, and possible consequences to embryonic growth were publicly debated. This is the topical background of the poem "Cloud upon Cloud" in *The Enigmatic Obstacles* (1961):

> Cloud upon cloud
> of underground fire—
> Extermination clouds
> of hate and abstractions—
> And we who are living, still breathing
> remembering another life.
> But this is our life:
> strontium and disgust.
> And the contagion—kept secret—
> that is spreading, that has already penetrated us!
> divided us from ourselves, divided
> the hands from the head, body and sex
> from the heart, the man from the woman
> as east from west—
>
> Cloud upon cloud
>
> What a miracle that this world within the world
> still radiates its beam,
> that womb, breast and lips
> still catch the weak echo

and eyes meet:
the secret motive
for another life.

But this is our life: strontium and disgust.
Caesium and emptiness.
Shut rocks, closed spaces.
Hate against hate.
An atmosphere that doesn't breathe,
a fabricated desert atmosphere.

The trees, the animals pine away as we do
in this encroaching wilderness—

Cloud upon cloud
of underground fire—
Extermination clouds
of hate and abstractions—
This is our life.
While the ash is falling, falling . . .[14]

Irresponsible technology, the Cold War, and the spiritual torpor
and alienation of modern man are here seen as symptoms of
the same disease affecting all aspects of existence on earth. Still
breathing, inhaling the poisoned air, we can only remember
what life once used to be like, the life sustained by unpolluted
elements. Sjöstrand also senses a pollution of the very source and
spring of life, love, and protests against the impersonal mechani-
zation of sexuality, against what T. S. Eliot, in his essay on
Baudelaire, called "the natural, 'life-giving,' cheery automatism
of the modern world . . . sexual operation [as something] analogous to Kruschen Salts."[15] When, in Sjöstrand's words, "body
and sex" are divided "from the heart," "the man" is also divided
"from the woman." We find a similar connection between heart-
less sexuality and environmental pollution in one of the poems
in his 1967 collection: an allusion to *The American Nude* is
followed by the lines:

The lament of the flesh on the lit streets, the free,
contaminated fields.[16]

The original word for "contaminated" is "biocidbelagd," *i.e.* covered with biocides, with killers of life.

Still the eternal miracle is perpetually repeated: the conception of new life through love, of a new human universe growing in the womb, emitting its benign radiation in the face of man-made death rays. And true love is still possible—"and eyes meet"' —though the elements of life have turned into "strontium and disgust / Caesium and emptiness."

The poem ends on a note of despair presaging doom and destruction. And like Eliot, Sjöstrand foresees the end of the world not as a "bang" but as a slow, inexorable extinguishing of life: "While the ash is falling, falling...." The same feeling of a life and a world wasting away is voiced in another poem in *The Enigmatic Obstacles*, "After us":

> After us only the traces of a quenched
> camp fire, clinkers, refuse,
> combustion products, reflections
> of a life that was...[17]

The collection as a whole is not pessimistic, however. Sjöstrand is never a pessimist. He often lives and writes in a mood of apprehension of imminent crises and disasters, but the vital forces always in the end outweigh the powers of destruction and despair—seem, in fact, to feed on these very powers. In *The Enigmatic Obstacles* the hope for the future is still attached to traditionally Christian beliefs though Sjöstrand's interpretation of the character of the Saviour is rather unorthodox, as in the untitled poem beginning "A new heaven, a new earth."[18]

In the early 1960's Sjöstrand went through a period of deep depression reflected in *A Winter in the North* (1963), but as his confidence in life returned, his faith in survival and a future for the world also returned, now liberated from the bonds of traditional Christian theology, free to express itself in new images and bold symbols. Christ as Aquarius, as the Water Carrier, is the central symbol in his 1967 collection, *In the Sign of Aquarius*, perhaps his most important book. With its reference to astrology and calendaric symbolism, the Water Carrier connects Sjöstrand's speculation with esoteric doctrines and philosophies of history which flourished during and after the First

World War. And with its reference to the element of water Aquarius connects Sjöstrand's futurological poetry with a central environmental issue and with the deepest springs of his own creativity.

III *The Aquarius Symbolism*

The title of Sjöstrand's collection *In the Sign of Aquarius* may appear puzzling to those not versed in astrology though the name of Aquarius is well known. It is one of the twelve signs or houses of the Zodiac through which the sun passes on its yearly path around the ecliptic—that is to say, the cyclical movement which forms the foundation for all astrological systems. But the Zodiac also measures periods of time greater than the ordinary solar year. Annus Magnus, the great year, was the name given in the ancient world to the 27,000-year period which constitutes the epoch for the cyclical movement, backwards through the twelve signs, of the point of the vernal equinox. That World Year, or Platonic Year as it was sometimes called, was divided into twelve months, each having a full 2,000 years, and every month took its name from the sign in which the spring-point fell during the two-thousand-year period in question. At the time of Christ's birth the world month of Pisces, the Fish, began, and by that method of reckoning, time will soon enter the sign of Aquarius.

Up to this point we have been dealing with indisputable facts about which both astronomers and astrologers can be in agreement. The procession of the spring-point was known already to the ancient Babylonian astronomers and modern scientists have only contributed more exact methods of calculation. But the idea that the passage from one heavenly month to another will mark a turning point in world history, and that every epoch of 2,000 years will have a particular character which stands in relation to its heavenly sign, is, of course, like every other attempt to discern pattern and rhythm in historical appearance, a highly disputable question. Nevertheless, it is a form of interpretation with a long history. It was not only for Christianity that the time of Christ's birth marked a turning point in history. In the ancient world, particularly in Rome, the hope and belief in an imminent social and cultural regeneration had been gaining impetus throughout the previous century. Poets dreamed and wrote about a new golden age and Caesar Augustus with his Pax Romana was thought to have fulfilled these expectations when he founded the temporal Roman imperium.

The best known expression of this idea in pagan Roman literature is of course Virgil's fourth *Eclogue*, the so-called "Messianic" eclogue:

> Ultima Cumaei venit iam carminis aetas;
> magnus ab integro saeclorum nascitur ordo.

(In Fairclough's prose translation: "Now is come the last age of the song of Cumae; the great line of the centuries begins anew."[19]) The poet also prophesies the birth of a divine child under whose reign the golden age will return to earth. Owing to the similarities between Virgil's words and those of Isaiah in his messianic prophecy, the child in the fourth *Eclogue* was identified with Christ himself—an identification which smoothed out the gap between the pagan and the Christian empire. The contemporaneity on earth of Christ and Caesar Augustus was considered not a coincidence but a twofold inauguration of the new dispensation in the sign of Pisces.

It is not hard to understand how philosophers of history since the early Middle Ages have linked together the factual historic events at the beginning of our era with the astronomical fact that the point of the vernal equinox at the same time moved into the sign of Pisces. The fish, as is well known, was one of the most widespread symbols for Christ, who called fishermen to be his disciples and whose initials in Greek form the word for fish, *Ichthýs: Iesos Christos Theou Yios Soter*, Jesus Christ, the Son of God, Saviour. Now, if the beginning of the month of Pisces marked a historical, political, and religious turning-point, may we not expect corresponding revolutions at its end? May not the Christian era, possibly soon to pass away with the month of Pisces, be followed by a new era the character of which will be determined by Aquarius, whoever he may be? Astrologically-minded philosophers of history have so speculated, and from their speculations Sjöstrand has drawn some important elements in his poetry of the sixties.

There have of course been many versions of the cyclical view of historical development, and as we have seen, the idea that we now find ourselves at the end of a historical epoch was presented with great force by Spengler. But a source which according to Sjöstrand's own statement produced a more direct stimulus was Jung's treatise *Aion* (1951), in which the Christian fish symbolism and its historical meaning is exhaustively handled. In his usual manner, Jung combines in this book learned, scientific documentation with bold psychological hypotheses and sweeping historical syntheses. Without a doubt the rationalist in Sjöstrand remains skeptical before much of this, but when, on major points, he shares Jung's intuitive experience of history it is justifiable to interpret Sjöstrand's fish symbolism in the light of *Aion*.

In Jung's exposition the pictorial quality of the zodiacal sign Pisces plays an important role. First, we should notice that the sign consists of two fishes, symbolizing an antithesis:

Since the Fishes stand for mother and son, the mythological tragedy of the son's early death and resurrection is already implicit in them. Being the twelfth sign of the Zodiac, Pisces denotes the end of the astrological year and also a new beginning. This characteristic coincides with the claim of Christianity to be the beginning and end of all things, and with its eschatological expectation of the end of the world and the coming of God's kingdom. Thus the astrological characteristics of the fish contain essential components of the Christian myth; first, the cross; second, the moral conflict and its splitting into the figures of Christ and Antichrist; third, the motif of the son of a virgin; fourth, the classical mother-son tragedy; fifth, the danger at birth; and sixth, the saviour and bringer of healing. It is therefore not beside the point to relate the designation of Christ as a fish to the new aeon then dawning. If this relationship existed even in antiquity, it must obviously have been a tacit assumption or one that was purposely kept secret; for, to my knowledge, there is no evidence in the old literature that the Christian fish symbolism was derived from the Zodiac.[20]

Now, while Christ was symbolized by a single fish, the astrological sign consists of two fishes. As a rule they are depicted one above the other and turned in opposite directions, and that relation becomes for Jung, as for Sjöstrand, a symbol of the inner division between the spiritual and the worldly in the

Christian view of things, in endless theological strife and devastating wars in the name of Christendom. Jung also toys with the idea that the center of the sign constitutes the symbolic equivalent of the midpoint of the period, that is to say, the Renaissance:

The northerly, or easterly fish, which the spring-point entered at about the beginning of our era, is joined to the southerly, or westerly, fish by the so-called commissure. This consists of a band of weak stars forming the middle sector of the constellation, and the spring-point gradually moved along its southern edge. The point where the ecliptic intersects with the meridian between the two fishes coincides roughly with the sixteenth century, the time of the Reformation, which as we know is so extraordinarily important for the history of Western symbols. Since then the spring-point has moved along the southern edge of the second fish, and will enter Aquarius in the course of the third millennium. Astrologically interpreted, the designation of Christ as one of the fishes identifies him with the first fish, the vertical one. Christ is followed by the Antichrist, at the end of time. The beginning of the enantiodromia would fall, logically, midway between the two fishes. We have seen that this is so. The time of the Renaissance begins in the immediate vicinity of the second fish, and with it comes that spirit which culminates in the modern age.[21]

In the Renaissance, it is true, one can see a turning to the past, to ancient, pre-Christian culture, and an openness to the future, the beginnings of the scientific development which now triumphs. Dante, the neo-Platonic philosophers of Florence and Ferrara, Copernicus and Galileo, all belong to the same epoch, which certainly was extremely dynamic but not dualistic as was the Middle Ages with its, as least in theory, absolute boundaries between the earthly and the heavenly, or as was the age of Rationalism, from the beginning of the eighteenth century up to our own time, with its absolute boundaries between what can and what cannot be rationally comprehended. During the Renaissance, man had a brief breathing space when he could develop his whole being in freedom before the split in the eon of Pisces again prevailed. This is, certainly, an extremely simplified and schematized description of history which, however, does explain something of the attraction which the Renaissance manifestly holds for Sjöstrand. In his poetry he eagerly returns to these rich centuries as, in his travels, he eagerly tries to get away to the lands of the Mediterranean where the culture of the Renaissance still remains, in the form of monuments and a living tradition.

On this view, consequently, the era of Pisces has a precise character. But who is Aquarius? Jung speaks more generally about what is to be expected during the impending world-month: the union of opposites:

If, as seems probable, the aeon of the fishes is ruled by the archetypal motif of the hostile brothers, then the approach of the next Platonic month, namely Aquarius, will constellate the problem of the union of opposites. It will then no longer be possible to write off evil as the mere privation of good; its real existence will have to be recognized.[22]

Sjöstrand, too, foresees a time of strife when evil will be experienced as something very real, but his interpretation of the sign of Aquarius emphasizes the union and the hope of a better dispensation. In the pictorial representation of the Zodiac, Aquarius is a human figure who pours water out of an urn. As the point of the vernal equinox moves backwards through the Zodiac, Aquarius becomes the first human figure after a line of lower creatures: Pisces, Aries, Taurus. In Sjöstrand's poetry the new era is also referred to as the time of Man. Man will pour out the life-giving water over the earth. In the sign of Aquarius, also, there will be the union of opposites, between humanity and nations, between belief and knowledge, between spirit and matter, for in the microcosm of man all existence is contained. The time of Aquarius will, after a painful era of transition, be a new golden age of man on earth. This is the hope implicit in Sjöstrand's poetry.

It is a common belief that each period of global regeneration is heralded by some kind of apocalypse. Mankind has still not left Pisces, the sign of strife, and the immediate future presents itself for Sjöstrand as a time of suffering and hardship in expectation of a better world order which most of those now living perhaps will never reach or be capable of experiencing. Now according to Sjöstrand, it is the visionary poet's calling to anticipate and undergo these hardships symbolically in his inner life. As is clear at several points in his *Aquarius* collection, it has been produced under strong inner pressure and in an acute state of crisis. But out of chaos and despair emerges the New Knowledge.

The exact year when time moves into the sign of Aquarius depends on the kind of reckoning applied. Jung quotes as two extreme estimates the years 1997 and 2154.[23] If we accept the earlier date, the great change is indeed approaching quickly, and the sense of an imminent reversal of the whole world order permeates *In the Sign of Aquarius*. In the poem "The Study of Stress," for instance, the same phrase recurs three times: "In five minutes there'll be rapping on the door." Apprehension and expectation seem to balance each other in this premonition of an unknown visitor. The concluding lines of the poem reveal something of his identity: he is both the Water Carrier and the master of the New Knowledge:

> Before waters, which shall never more cease flowing
> *In five minutes there'll be rapping on the door*
> And he, the man of the complex numbers, shall open it.[24]

IV *On the Threshold of the Future*

Sjöstrand's attitude toward the Aquarius symbolism outlined above must not be understood too literally. However, the general feeling expressed by Jung and others that humanity stands on the threshold of a new era certainly corresponds to his personal experience, as does the view that the present era was inaugurated by the rise of Christianity. But the nature and characteristics of the new era can of course only be a matter of speculation, fear and hope.

The methods of current futurology cannot be applied to Sjöstrand's poetic approach to the future, at least not without important qualifications. The futurological forecasts, or "scenarios" as they are sometimes called, are always founded on historical data arranged so as to form graphic lines of development susceptible to mathematical analysis, the forecasts being the results of the application of the formulas thus obtained to the continuation of the lines into the future, *i.e.* they are deductions from and extrapolations on what is given and known, varying according to the data selected as most representative of the present and near past. Sjöstrand's view of the future, on the other hand, is essentially dialectic in a general, non-Marxist

sense, regarding decisive changes in history not as the mere
convergence of sociopolitical lines of development but as an
eruption of cumulative spiritual forces, of a new consciousness
which has gradually matured into articulate action. The passage
into the new era should be interpreted as a dialectic leap corresponding to the leap from the sign of Aries into that of Pisces
at the time of Christ's birth.

Again, it is doubtful to what extent these dialectics should
be taken literally in Sjöstrand's case. The most adequate approach
to his futurological poetry perhaps suggests itself as a parallel
to the English Metaphysical poetry of the seventeenth century.
How far Donne, for example, "believed" in the doctrine of
micro-macrocosmical relationships underlying much of his poetry,
is a question not only impossible to answer with any certainty
but largely irrelevant to the study of his poetry. It is quite
sufficient that he found that doctrine a rewarding means of
representing his inner experience in poetically effective imagery.
The same applies to Sjöstrand's Aquarius symbolism.

The essence of Sjöstrand's futurological speculation is contained in two comparatively short poems, both printed in the
Aquarius collection. The first is called "Time Entered the Sign
of Aquarius":

> Time entered the sign of Aquarius.
> The old metals rusted and melted.
> Where were the hard substances in the soul,
> wolfram, molybdenum, martensit?
>
> Time was short.
>
>   Feverishly we sought
> the formulae for the new alloys,
> registered on the plates of cloud chambers
> the tracks of charged particles, the smallest,
> the most fugitive, antimatter . . .
>
> We remembered—in the pause outside the sought
> field of force—that in this flesh
> Christ took his dwelling . . .
>
> In this flesh, which would dissolve in dew
> and melt away!

> Would Hamlet rise against the usurper,
> drive out the defiler? With firm decisiveness,
> more resilient than the known minerals,
> and the sought, unknown transurania?
>
> Time entered the sign of Aquarius.[25]

Using the terminology of Metaphysical poetry, one might say that this poem is built on a complex conceit integrating elements from four different fields: the Aquarius philosophy; contemporary science and technology; the theology of Incarnation; and the Renaissance drama of *Hamlet*.

The element derived from science and technology clearly links up with Sjöstrand's ideas on a New Knowledge—the poem of that name follows immediately after the present one in the collection. As discussed in a previous chapter, the protagonist in "The New Knowledge" is an astronomer breaking into a new dimension of knowledge. Here the "we" are scientists busy on the one hand developing new metallic alloys demanded by modern technology—molybdenum and martensit are components in steel alloys used for instance in space ships—and on the other hand establishing the actual existence of that elusive thing antimatter, a thing which is neither the thing in itself nor the thing to us. The tiniest particles of such antimatter have been observed in laboratory experiments, confirming, it seems, the theory that there exists a whole universe equivalent to "our" universe only inverted in such a way that what is electrically positive in matter is negative in antimatter and vice versa. In a collision between bodies of matter and antimatter, both are instantaneously and completely transformed into energy leaving no trace behind neither material nor antimaterial.

The basis for a symbolical interpretation of the metals in Sjöstrand's poem is given by the line, "Where were the hard substances in the soul." As technology needs new alloys to withstand the strains of space travel and the taming of nuclear energy, so man, entering the new age of such techniques, needs inner qualities to fortify himself against the strains of life in that age. And the search for particles of antimatter seems, on the symbolical level, to stand for the search for that new spirit or consciousness which alone may save the world—though it may

explode when brought in contact with the prevailing spirit of
the twentieth century: a warning that the transition into the
new era is likely to become a period of violent wars and revolutions. The discovery of antimatter may also be taken, Sjöstrand
seems to mean, as an argument in favor of the idea that ultimate
reality is spiritual. For the common denominator of matter and
antimatter is the polarity between opposite charges, *i.e.* a pure
abstraction to be encompassed only in a theory postulating something more elementary than the so-called "elementary" particles,
that something which Sjöstrand also calls "the hidden music."

The theme of time running short recurs in this poem, too. We
must press for the discoveries necessary for survival in the new
era, we must "redeem the time," to use a phrase of St. Paul's.
For as Sjöstrand put it in "The Study of Stress," "In five minutes
there'll be rapping on the door."[26]

The third component of the central conceit of the poem is the
Incarnation: "that in this flesh / Christ took his dwelling." While
searching for the antimaterial world we must not forget that
the divinity of man is to be realized also in the known world
of flesh and blood. In the sign of Aquarius man will not change
physically. He will be the same, only with a renewed awareness
of his human dignity.

At this point the poet is struck by the irony of the idea. The
flesh, in which Christ took his dwelling, is notorious for its
frailty, as often felt to be an unbearable burden as the glory of
the lord of creation. Hamlet's lament springs to the poet's mind,
the protest against the law forbidding the slaughtering of that
flesh which in any case is doomed to decay and destruction.

The allusion to *Hamlet* serves not only the purpose of ironic
contrast, however. As a typical Renaissance man, Hamlet stands
for that crucial period in the era of Pisces when the dualism
of the Christian view of man and the world was first rejected
in favor of the conception of an integrated *homo dei*. But Hamlet's rejection of the old world order was only half-hearted, and
beset by doubts and weakness he failed to take action. Now,
at the next crucial point in history, the question is: will the
Hamlets of the dawning age of Aquarius take the right action,
will they let themselves be guided by the firm purpose which
their Renaissance ancestor so sadly lacked? And the "defiler" to

be driven out is of course Hamlet's mother Queen Gertrude, representing the obscenity of sexuality divorced from love, which is one of Sjöstrand's recurrent complaints against contemporary Western society.

The whole poem, "Time Entered the Sign of Aquarius," has the character of a question. Contained within the frame of the title line, which both opens and concludes the piece, are two sentences ending with a question mark, and within them are two long sentences expressing a feverish search and a doubtful memory. Thus the very form of the poem suggests the mixed feeling of feverish hope, longing, fear, doubt, and resolve that must characterize man facing the new era. Since Sjöstrand does not preach a futurological gospel, nor propound a philosophy of history, but gives poetic shape and voice to his emotional experience of man's prospects on earth, it is only natural that the tone should vary from one poem to another. The same set of ideas and experiences may as well lead to pessimism and despair as to optimism and hope. One poem in which hope and affirmation prevail and where most of Sjöstrand's futurological themes converge is "Each Particle Has the Whole Universe for its Field of Activity":

On a bitter country lane, among feverous fish,
the endless retinue of cripples and cattle,
he abandons the circle for the orb and for the Sphere.

On a bitter country lane, where the words have become
syllables of dust, phrases
of frost and the scorching sun,

the aching sleepless thoughts have been touched
by the incomprehensible depths: as by galaxies
heard, never seen. Freshwater—

Freshwater, Ploughland, Implements, Schools—
Although the list still sounds like a rattle,
a wooden clapper—his eyes still only see

the Destroyer's white mules, a down-turned setsquare;
the broken terrestrial chain of friends
and habits, is healed. He is reunited

with the millions of years and the country lane, with the Cosmos.
He will soon, beyond the feverous fish,
see anew: the Irrigation System,

the Housebuilding Projects, the original sign
of the Living Fish: he has already said yes.[27]

The tendency and meaning of this poem can without great
difficulty be fixed in broad outline, but the interpretation of the
separate images must be tentative and leave room for different
possibilities. The "he" of the poem may well be taken as a
representative of all men on the border between the two world-
months who are still caught in the present world order but
reach out toward the new.

The first image, the bitter country lane with the train of
cripples and cattle, makes concrete reference, for example, to an
Indian village where the people are restricted to a stunted and
impoverished life in the midst of their holy cows. But "among
feverous fish" breaks the unity of the concrete image. By means
of the introduction of the fish symbol the country lane takes
on a wider allusion: it is the road down which mankind has
wandered during the two-thousand-year era which is soon to
end. It is a country lane to the side of the great highway
through the ages, whether it be the great oriental philosophic
and religious tradition or the open and free spirit we meet in
Greek culture and in the Renaissance. With this interpretation
the train of cripples becomes not only an image of the physical
distress in the impoverished parts of the world but also an image
of a limited, dogmatic religious, or positivistic view of life which
has crippled mankind. And the fish, whose sign rules over this
wandering on the side-road, are "feverous," that is, sick, over-
heated, just as Sjöstrand, like Jung, considers the Christian era
to be. But "feverous" most likely also alludes to the condition in
which the poem was conceived, a kind of feverish vision in which
images from outer reality blended with symbols from the
inner being.

The poem then suggests the possibility of mankind's escape
from the train of cripples, from the constricting and debilitating
aspects of contemporary society and culture, and of his reunion

with an older tradition—*i.e.* his passing from the sign of Pisces to the sign of Aquarius.

The first step in the new direction consists of abandoning "the circle for the orb and for the Sphere," and it is no accident that geometric symbols hold this prominent place. In the mathematical, scientific development of recent years, Sjöstrand sees the germ of an entirely new knowledge of the world, a knowledge the human content of which we are only beginning to imagine. The symbols also allude, of course, to the abandonment by space physicists and cosmologists of Euclidean plane geometry in favor of spherical geometry without which Einstein's revolution would not have been possible. This transition, from a description of space in terms of three flat dimensions to one in terms of curvature and many dimensions, stands therefore in the poem for the difficulty and, in general, openness of the world picture of the new physics: the rectilinear universe has been exchanged for one curved, absolute time for relative time, the fixed idea of matter for fields of forces, and so on.

In the second stanza the geometric symbols are exchanged for "words," "syllables," and "phrases." The scientist has led the way in the revolt against the flat world picture; the poet follows. Like most poets in our time, Sjöstrand suffers from a sense of the impotence of words; they have been blasted and decomposed to "syllables of dust," deprived of their possibilities for a higher and deeper direction. But as the spherical thinking opened a new perspective for physics, so for poets the new sciences of man have opened new dimensions: the inconceivable depths in the cosmos around us and in man's own inner being. Biochemistry and depth psychology have brought about a revolution in the view of man as sweeping as the view of modern astronomy concerning the cosmos. The light of the distant galaxies which does not reach us visibly but can still be received by the radio telescope appears in the poem as an example and, at the same time, a symbol of the abysses in time and space which conceal themselves outside us and within us.

Regeneration from the depths leads up to the word "Freshwater" which occurs twice in succeeding lines in the middle of the poem: symbolically it is the life-giving water of Aquarius which will be poured out over the earth, but the words also have

as immediately a concrete sense as the following words: "Ploughland, Implements, Schools." Freshwater: the water which will
make the deserts of the earth fruitful; Ploughland: the good earth
which will send bread to the hungry of the earth, the antithesis of
the "contaminated fields" discussed above; Implements: the
technology which is man's servant, not his master; Schools: en-
lightenment and education for everyone on earth, as well as a
new knowledge and a new wisdom. That sounds like a global
project for underdeveloped countries, and so it is in its own way.
But the fine words have become a "list." They "sound like a
rattle, / a wooden clapper." They echo hollowly, they are felt
to be empty and meaningless before the hard reality they cannot
yet conquer. But nevertheless they signify something which has
real worth, for their realization is a way of abandoning the
bitter country lane.

When Sjöstrand is now and then accused of that deadly sin
of today, an insufficient engagement in the social and political
problems of mankind, it is partially due to an incomplete understanding of the content of his latest poetry, and partially to his
distaste for a single position on any question. The speaker in the
poem, who lives on the border between two periods of time, is
active in working for a better world but is still not able to see
clearly the purpose of his work. His eyes still only see "the
Destroyer's white mules, a down-turned setsquare." These images
compress an entire critique of culture. A prominent attribute
of mules, that product of man's ingenious experiments in breed-
ing, is their sterility. Though whiteness is most immediately
associated with purity and holiness, one could interpret the
phrase "the Destroyer's white mules" to mean man's destructive
intrusion into the life of nature, and the espousal by certain
religious views of sterility and chastity as something holy, that
is to say the antinatural element in Christian culture, its ascetic
turning away from life. The setsquare may well be thought of
as standing for modern technology, which here points down
toward annihilation and death instead of up toward infinity.
The new technology should be a blessing, something which leads
mankind upwards, but instead it furnishes destructive weapons
of increasing effectiveness.

But the hopelessness and despair are not in vain. Those who

stand right in the midst of the battle for a new and better world
are easily tempted by mistrust and fail to see that "the broken
terrestrial chain of friends / and habits, is healed." The chain
which is broken is the chain of human solidarity and affinity
but also the chain which unites mankind with the cosmic world
order. In the older tradition, the golden chain was the image
of universal hierarchy in which every created thing had its place
and function assigned by God, and Sjöstrand's meaning seems
to be that only when that broken chain is made whole can the
human bond be whole. For whoever is restored to his correct
relation with friends and habits is also "reunited / with the
millions of years and the country lane, with the Cosmos."

Toward its end the poem opens out into prophecy. Mankind,
awakened but still groping in darkness, will soon see Pisces
superseded by Aquarius: "the Irrigation System, / the Housebuilding Projects, the original sign / of the Living Fish." That
will be an era of reconstruction of the resources of the earth,
of spiritual values. And here, not in the past 2,000 years of
Christendom, will the Living Fish, Christ, be at home. The fish
as a symbol of Christ has already been commented on, so here
the only point to stress is that the Living Fish is *one* in contrast
to the "feverous fish," who form a pair of opposites. The new
age will bring about a union of opposites, it will be an eon of
peace instead of strife.

Finally, the title of the poem, "Each Particle Has the Whole
Universe for its Field of Activity." As one reviewer noted, the
title could "do as the heading for a chapter on field theory in
a textbook on physics."[28] That a sentence with such direct
scientific associations serves as the title for a poem about the
historical and social situation of mankind palpably shows how
the two spheres coincide for Sjöstrand. As every moving particle
can be fixed only in relation to the whole universe, so the individual human being can only be identified and have meaning in
relation to all of mankind and its history. That is the analogy
which is in the title. Further, the analogy expresses a kind of
identity that has often been considered in this book: the identity
of the physical and the spiritual universe which are only two
aspects or forms of the same thing.

V *Time of Man*

In Sjöstrand's utopian society of the world month to come, Aquarius will not be the sole ruler. His male, life-giving reign will be shared by Hagia Sophia, the female principle of Holy Wisdom. And their union will be a pattern for a humanity liberated and reconciled to itself. In the sign of Aquarius, man will come into his own. Sjöstrand emphasizes his conviction that the complete and integrated humanity is a union of male and female by putting a male human figure in the title of his collection *In the Sign of Aquarius* while opening the book with a poem called "Wisdom" invoking an ancient goddess:

I

Lamenting, in the cave of ambiguous confession, in the
            secret darkness apart . . .
Upright, in the regained light of day, close by the olive
            tree. (With the sparkling cells, the playing
            thoughts, protected by the shining helmet!)

You saw Her triumphal coach, drawn by white runners, at a
            court in Ferrara.
But the olive sprig was broken, for the true Minerva:
            the wind of Wisdom, Hagia Sophia!

II

And where is Her life-giving breath and calling now?
In the inquiring thought, in the possible city,
            at the heart of the perpetually reborn activity;
where the eight-fold way opens out, in the fragments of
            created matter, the sought genetic code;
in the mutations of the human sea, that inner sea which
            also heaves towards the moon, some degrees
            warmer: with us—your co-creators, O God![29]

In the third line we find ourselves transported to the Renaissance, that period in the month of Pisces when the human spirit was temporarily freed from its dogmatic fetters. The image of Minerva's triumph at the court of Ferrara is evoked, and that classical goddess of wisdom stands for the rediscovered free spirit of antiquity. The concluding part of the poem asks what place in our time the Minerva of antiquity and of the Renaissance can have. Since Minerva is also the patroness of art, the concluding lines may be seen as a program for poetry in our time. For Sjöstrand, the esthetics of *l'art pour l'art* has played out its role. The role of art is now, in the first place, to communicate, interpret, and shape the knowledge, insights, and experiences which wash over us from the different branches of natural and social sciences, but the meaning and mutual relations of which slip from the hands of highly specialized experts. In the enumeration of the areas where the life-giving breath of wisdom can now be apprehended, several of the themes of the collection are anticipated. "The possible city," for example, is related to the "Housebuilding Projects" in "Each Particle..." And the "eight-fold way" has a double reference: in part it refers to the way of Buddhism to insight and virtue which points forward to a series of elements of Indian philosophy and religion in the collection, in part to an advanced theory of elementary particle physics. And in the parallelling of the outer and inner ocean, both subject to the power of the moon, the central idea of the collection is suggested, an idea which has already been discussed several times: outer, material, physical, biological reality has a corresponding inner, psychic, spiritual reality.

The final words, "with us—your co-creators, O God!," can again be linked to the Renaissance world of ideas, to the humanists' conception of *homo dei*. The era of Aquarius is "the time of man," as it is called in one poem,[30] and man is divine to the degree that he is creative, on all levels—in love, in science, in social-political life ("at the heart of the perpetually reborn activity")—and the paradigm for all this is artistic creation.

It is the divine, female figure of Wisdom who dominates the long poem "The Very Moment," beginning:

> Like a wave washing through the primary rocks themselves
> so She spoke within me,
> so Her being called forth the healing
> all-demanding Light[31]

It is She who—in a passage quoted before—leads the poet over "the decisive threshold—to the Poem, / thermonuclear energy, / the liberated Common Spirit." Psychologically she may be interpreted in the light of Jung's doctrine of the Anima of man, that is, the female principle inherent in his inmost being. Proceeding into the new era, man must rely on the natural, divine wisdom with which he is endowed since the dawn of creation. The present era has been one of alienation from both natural and spiritual life and a waste of both natural and spiritual resources. In the concluding words of "The Very Moment":

> After degradation (spilt water)
> the new trust.

The water that was spilt will now be purposefully poured out by Aquarius, and the new trust will be inspired by his queen and consort, Wisdom.

The central themes of the Aquarius poetry recur in Sjöstrand's latest collection, *The Dream is No Façade*. Its introductory poem, "Counter-Statements, Contrary Lights," again shows contemporary man poised on the threshold of the future, suffering, almost despairing, yet conscious of a different world to come, to be created by himself:

> The world waxed.
> Sorrow spread.
> In the hearts of men
> seeped mercury and apathy.
>
> But I thought: seasons, not years!
> Trees, not burnt, defoliated forests,
> millions of trees . . .[32]

Against the vision of pollution, waste, and degradation is set this belief in the possibilities of man, which forms the message of Östen Sjöstrand's work. The poem concludes:

> Man
> is not a blind alley
> among condemned tenement blocks
> and the seventh generation of computers.
> He is not a straying fly
> among rustling steppe grass

and myriads of luminous galaxies.
              With us
for the first time matter is entering
history.

Wake up from your shameful torpor!

In the hearts of men
seeped mercury and apathy.

Notes and References

Works cited below without author are, of course, Sjöstrand's own. The titles are given in the original Swedish, not, as in the text, in accepted or ad hoc English translations. For converting Swedish titles into English, see the bibliographical list of Sjöstrand's works below, where the details of publication are given.

Chapter One

1. *Fantasins nödvändighet*, p. 45. When not otherwise stated or indicated in the text or the following references, the sources of biographical information are the poet himself, his sister, Mrs. Maria Pettersson, Gothenburg, and the letters, photographs, and other personal documents they have placed at my disposal.
2. *Fantasins nödvändighet*, p. 51.
3. *Ibid.*, pp. 46 f.
4. *I vattumannens tecken*, p. 65.
5. *Fantasins nödvändighet*, p. 51.
6. Hillbäck, E., *Cirkusvagnen* (Stockholm, 1959).
7. *En vinter i Norden*, p. 35.
8. The review appeared in *Göteborgs Morgonpost*, June 18, 1947.
9. *Unio*, p. 20.
10. In *Göteborgs Morgonpost*, July 10, 1947.
11. *Unio*, p. 14.
12. *Ibid.*, p. 35.
13. "Vision och återkomst" is the title of Sjöstrand's essay on *Ash Wednesday*, published in *Ande och verklighet*, pp. 107–29.
14. Olof Lagercrantz in *Svenska Dagbladet*, 1949.
15. *Ande och verklighet*, p. 110.
16. *Ibid.*, pp. 20–21.
17. *Främmande mörker, främmande ljus*, p. 47.
18. "Återkomst," in *Hemlöshet och hem*, p. 58.
19. *Världen skapas varje dag*, pp. 18–19.
20. *De gåtfulla hindren*, p. 77.
21. *Ibid.*, pp. 78–79 (the poem "Skapelseordet").
22. *En vinter i Norden*, p. 20.
23. *Ibid.*, p. 23.
24. *Ibid.*, p. 29.

25. *Ibid.*, p. 50.
26. "Burnt Norton," III.
27. *En vinter i Norden*, pp. 92–93.
28. *Drömmen är ingen fasad*, pp. 15–16.
29. See above, p. 00.
30. *Drömmen är ingen fasad*, pp. 19–20. As early as 1960 Sjöstrand devoted one of the essays in *Världen skapas varje dag* to Robert Lowell, who, as is well known, is an ex-Catholic like Sjöstrand. See the interview with Lowell in *The Review* (26, 1971), which was published in Swedish translation in *Lyrikvännen* (2, 1972).
31. See for instance "Den enda stunden" ("The Very Moment"), in *I vattumannens tecken*, pp. 31 ff.
32. *Ibid.*, p. 42.
33. See above, p. xx.
34. *Drömmen är ingen fasad*, pp. 28, 30.
35. *Ibid.*, p. 10.
36. Quoted from the paperback ed. (London, Pan Books, 1966), p. 260 (Part II, 11).
37. *I vattumannens tecken*, p. 22.

Chapter Two

1. *Fantasins nödvändighet*, p. 51.
2. *Ibid.*, p. 48.
3. *Ibid.*, p. 86.
4. *Ibid.*, pp. 127–30.
5. The following works seem representative: Calvin S. Brown, *Music and Literature. A Comparison of the Arts* (Athens, Ga., 1948); by the same author, *Tones into Words. Musical Compositions as Subjects of Poetry* (Athens, Ga., 1953); Johannes Mittenzwei, *Das Musikalische in der Literatur. Ein Überblick von Gottfried von Strassburg bis Brecht* (Halle, 1962).
6. *Fantasins nödvändighet*, pp. 68, 69 f.
7. *Claude Debussy*, Stockholm, 1948, p. 94.
8. *Ibid.*, p. 125.
9. Debussy's water symbolism is expounded in a rather esoteric way by Vladimir Jankélévitch in *Debussy et le Mystère* (Neuchatel, 1949), especially pp. 47–54.
10. *Invigelse*, p. 41.
11. *The Piano Works of Claude Debussy*, New York, 1950, p. 156.
12. *Ibid.*, p. 30.
13. *Unio*, p. 38 f.
14. *Dikter mellan midnatt och gryning*, p. 11.
15. For a summary of the legend, see any edition of the *Grand*

Larousse encyclopedia, s.v. Ys. Lalo's opera was performed a hundred times in Paris within thirteen months of its première in April, 1888. See A. Loewenberg, *Annals of Opera*, vol. I, 2nd ed. (Genève, 1955), col. 1132.

16. Schmitz, *op. cit.*, p. 155.

17. *Unio*, p. 17; *Invigelse*, pp. 55, 67; *En vinter i Norden*, p. 79; *I vattumannens tecken*, p. 59.

18. *Dikter mellan midnatt och gryning*, p. 20.

19. Schmitz, *op. cit.*, p. 156.

20. *Fantasins nödvändighet*, p. 100.

21. Valéry, P., "Fragments des mémoires d'un Poème," in Valéry's *Variété*, vol. V (Paris, 1945), p. 92. For a general discussion of this subject, see W. N. Ince, *The Poetic Theory of Paul Valéry* (Leicester, 1961), pp. 117 ff.

22. Valéry, p. 94.

23. *Fantasins nödvändighet*, p. 70.

24. *Ibid.*, p. 91.

25. This according to Sjöstrand himself.

26. *Fantasins nödvändighet*, pp. 92 f.

27. *Ibid.*, pp. 94 f.

28. *Ibid.*, p. 96.

29. Copies of the piano score are available at Nordiska Musikförlaget, Stockholm.

30. *Fantasins nödvändighet*, p. 95.

31. *Nutida musik*, vol. 10, no. 3/4 (Stockholm, 1966/67), p. 6.

32. *Nutida musik*, vol. 2, no. 5 (1958/59), pp. 17 f. With slight alterations reprinted in Sjöstrand's *Världen skapas varje dag*, pp. 35–40.

33. *En vinter i Norden*, p. 70.

34. *Fantasins nödvändighet*, p. 101.

35. *Ibid.*, p. 106, where Sjöstrand refers to Kaufmann without saying whether he read him before or after the concert. Kaufmann's essay, translated from the German original into Swedish, appeared in *Nutida musik*, vol. 8, no. 5/6 (1965), pp. 154–59. An English version of the same essay goes with the phonograph recording of Ligeti's *Requiem* issued by Heliodor/Wergo (2549 011). Ligeti's work and his place in musical life in Sweden is described in two books by O. Nordwall: *Det omöjligas konst — Anteckningar kring György Ligetis musik* (Norstedts, Stockholm, 1966); and *Ligeti-dokument* (same publ., 1968).

36. *Fantasins nödvändighet*, p. 106.

37. See Thomas Mann, *Doctor Faustus*, Engl. transl. by Lowe-Porter, pp. 485 ff. Cf. Gunilla Bergsten, *Thomas Mann's Doctor Faus-*

tus. The Sources and Structure of the Novel (Univ. of Chicago Press, 69), pp. 179–200.

38. *I vattumannens tecken*, pp. 24–27.

39. *Fantasins nödvändighet*, p. 105.

40. Sjöstrand read Pausanias in a German translation ed. by E. Meyer, Zürich (Atlantis Verlag), 1954.

41. Sjöstrand had come across the figure of Abraxas not only in pictorial representations but also in "Absentia animi," one of the most celebrated poems by Gunnar Ekelöf. The Abraxas theme in that poem and its sources in ancient tradition have been studied by G. Bergsten in "Abraxas. Ett motiv hos Hermann Hesse och Gunnar Ekelöf," *Samlaren* vol. 85 (Uppsala, 1964), pp. 5–18.

42. Information concerning the genesis of *In Principio* has kindly been supplied by both Bäck and Sjöstrand.

43. *Nutida musik*, vol. 13 (1969/70), no. 4, pp. 9–10.

44. *Ibid.*, p. 2. *Världen skapas varje dag*, pp. 67–73.

45. *In Principio* has been published as a phonograph record by Sveriges Radios förlag, Stockholm. (SR 20–1)

46. *Invigelse*, p. 55.

Chapter Three

1. Koestler, A., *The Ghost in the Machine* (London, 1967), pp. xii f.

2. *Ibid.*, p. xii.

3. Schrödinger, E., *Science and Humanism. Physics in Our Time* (Cambridge, 1951), p. 4.

4. See the prefatory note to *Balthazar*, the second part of *The Alexandria Quartet* (London, 1958).

5. Pettersson, H., *Atomernas sprängning. En studie i modern alkemi* (Stockholm, 1927).

6. *I vattumannens tecken*, pp. 39, 78, 96.

7. *Invigelse*, p. 67; republished in *I vattumannens tecken*, p. 61.

8. In *Utsikt* (vol. 3, 1950), pp. 23 f.

9. *The Collected Works of C. G. Jung*, vol. 14: *Mysterium Coniunctionis* (New York, 1963), pp. 48 f.; 272.

10. Stagnelius, E. J., *Samlade skrifter* (Stockholm, 1911–19), vol. II, pp. 178 ff., and the commentary (vol. V, pp. 201 f.), which Sjöstrand studied carefully.

11. In *Utsikt* (vol. 2, no. 1, 1949), p. 21. One poem in *Unio* is entitled "Heraclitean Wisdom" (p. 53).

12. Heisenberg, W., *Physics and Philosophy. The Revolution in Modern Science* (London, 1959), p. 61.

13. *Utsikt* (vol. 2, no. 1, 1949), p. 21.

14. *Ibid.*

15. *E.g., Drömmen är ingen fasad,* pp. 9, 28.

16. *I vattumannens tecken,* p. 103. The quotation is from Heraclitus's *On the Universe,* XLV (Loeb Class. Library, transl. W. H. S. Jones; Jones has "harp" instead of "lyre" which, however, is the literal rendering of the Greek original).

17. *I vattumannens tecken,* p. 37.

18. Schrödinger, E., *Mind and Matter* (Cambridge, 1958), p. 38.

19. *Ibid.,* pp. 54 f.

20. *Fantasins nödvändighet,* p. 54.

21. Pettersson, H., *Oceanografi* (Stockholm, 1939); *Djuphavens gåtor* (Stockholm, 1943).

22. *Invigelse,* p. 51.

23. *Ibid.,* p. 52.

24. Cf. Pettersson, *Oceanografi,* pp. 58–62.

25. *Invigelse,* p. 54; republished in *I vattumannens tecken,* p. 60.

26. *Invigelse,* p. 55.

27. Gothenburg, 1934.

28. *Unio,* p. 15.

29. *I vattumannens tecken,* pp. 56 f.

30. Brain, R., *The Nature of Experience* (London, 1959), pp. 25–47.

31. See for instance the symposium *Theories of the Mind,* ed. by J. M. Scher (New York, 1962).

32. This summary is H. Hoijer's in his paper "The Sapir-Whorf Hypothesis," in *The American Anthropologist: Language and Culture.* Proceedings of a Conference on the Interrelations of Language and Other Aspects of Culture, ed. by H. Hoijer (Chicago, 1954), p. 93.

33. The quotations are from R. Schlapp's translation of Heitler's *Man and Science* (Edinburgh, 1963), p. 94.

34. *Ibid.,* p. 99.

35. *Ibid.,* pp. 50–52.

36. *Ibid.,* p. 100.

37. Bohm, D., in *Towards a Theoretical Biology,* 2. Sketches. A symposium ed. by C. H. Waddington (Edinburgh, 1969), pp. 46 f.

38. Heitler, p. 100.

39. See below, p. xxx.

40. *I vattumannens tecken,* p. 32.

41. *Ibid.,* pp. 58–59.

42. *Fantasins nödvändighet,* p. 98.

43. Wheeler, J. A., *Geometrodynamics* (New York, 1962). (Italian Physical Society: *Topics of Modern Physics,* vol. 1), p. xi.

44. *Ibid.,* p. 68.

45. *Ibid.*
46. *Ibid.*, p. 67.
47. *Ibid.* Cf. *Fantasins nödvändighet*, p. 100.
48. Cambridge, Mass., 1952. Chapter 1:3, "Music and Philosophy."
Sjöstrand probably read the Swedish translation: Paul Hindemith,
Musik i vår tid (Stockholm, 1956), pp. 19–23.
49. *Fantasins nödvändighet*, p. 99.
50. *Srimad Bhagavatam. The Wisdom of God*, translated by S.
Prabhanavanda (New York, 1943), p. 42.
51. *A Source Book in Indian Philosophy*, ed. by S. Radhakrishnan
and Ch. A. Moore (Princeton, 1957), p. 60.
52. Wheeler, p. 236.
53. *Fantasins nödvändighet*, p. 99.
54. *Ibid.*, p. 100.
55. Bake, A., "Indische Musik," in *Die Musik in Geschichte und
Gegenwart*, ed. by F. Blume, vol. 6 (Kassel, 1957), p. 1156. Sjöstrand's
chief source of knowledge was A. H. Fox Strangways, *The Music of
Hindostan* (Oxford, 1914).
56. *I vattumannens tecken*, p. 103.
57. Hoyle, F., *Galaxies, Nuclei and Quasars* (London, 1966);
Galaxer, atomkärnor och kvasarer (Stockholm, 1966).

Chapter Four

1. The concluding lines of *The Hollow Men* (1925).
2. Malmberg, B., *Dikter vid gränsen* (Stockholm, 1935), the poem
"Midnatt," IV.
3. Ekelöf, G., *Sent på jorden* (Stockholm, 1932, 1962), the poem
"dödstystnad från gult till svart."
4. See the facsimile edition of *The Waste Land*, ed. by Valerie
Eliot (London, 1971), p. 1.
5. Malmberg, B., *Ett stycke väg* (autobiography), (Stockholm,
1950), p. 206.
6. "A book of suicide" are Ekelöf's own words of *Late on Earth*
in his autobiographical essay "En outsiders väg" in *Promenader och
Utflykter* (Stockholm, 1963), p. 174.
7. Rimbaud, in letter to Paul Demeny of May 15, 1871.
8. *I vattumannens tecken*, p. 22. Cf. above ch. 1, the end.
9. These general ideas are to be found in many of C. G. Jung's
works, *e.g.* in the chapter "The Archetypes of the Collective Unconscious" in *The Psychology of the Unconscious* (*The Collected
Works of C. G. Jung*, vol. 7, 2nd ed., New York, 1966, pp. 90–113).
The timelessness of the unconscious is discussed *e.g.* in Jung's essay
on "The Tibetan Book of the Great Liberation" (*The Collected Works*,

vol. 11, 2nd ed. New York, 1963, pp. 490 f.) Jung's views on history will be discussed later in this chapter.

10. Eckehart, Sermon XIX, on Luke 21:31.

11. Among these poets were Karl Asplund, Hjalmar Gullberg, and Anders Österling.

12. Södergran, E., *Samlade dikter*, 2nd ed. (Stockholm, 1966), pp. 68, 76.

13. *Hemlöshet och hem*, p. 15.

14. *De gåtfulla hindren*, pp. 35 f.

15. Eliot, T. S., *Selected Essays*, 3rd ed. (London, 1951), p. 429.

16. *I vattumannens tecken*, p. 33.

17. *De gåtfulla hindren*, p. 61.

18. *Ibid.*, pp. 20 f.

19. *Virgil*, in Loeb Classical Library, vol. I, pp. 28 f.

20. Jung, C. G., *Aion* (*Collected Works*, vol. 9:II) (New York, 1959), pp. 114 f. Part of the quotation is in italics, here omitted.

21. *Ibid.*, pp. 93 f.

22. *Ibid.*, p. 87.

23. *Ibid.*, p. 94, note 84.

24. *I vattumannens tecken*, p. 45.

25. *Ibid.*, pp. 54 f.

26. *Ibid.*, p. 43.

27. *Ibid.*, pp. 19 f.

28. Hall, T., "Poesi och naturvetenskap," in *Svenska Dagbladet*, March 10, 1968.

29. *I vattumannens tecken*, p. 9.

30. *Ibid.*, p. 59.

31. *Ibid.*, p. 31.

32. *Drömmen är ingen fasad*, p. 9.

Selected Bibliography

WORKS OF ÖSTEN SJÖSTRAND

A. *Books and Pamphlets* (in chronological order)

Complete list up to 1973. When not otherwise stated the publisher is Bonniers, Stockholm. English titles are given in parentheses after each item.

Unio. En diktsvit. 1949. (*Unio. A Suite of Poems.*)
Invigelse. Dikter. 1950. (*Consecration. Poems.*)
Återvändo. Dikter. 1953. (*Return. Poems.*)
Dikter mellan midnatt och gryning. Privately printed, Gothenburg, 1954. (*Poems between Midnight and Dawn.*)
Ande och verklighet. 1954. (*Spirit and Reality. Essays.*)
Främmande mörker, främmande ljus. 1955. (*Strange Darkness, Strange Light. Poems.*)
80-tal. En lyrikantologi. 1956. (*1880's. An Anthology of Lyrical Poetry.*)
Där rosen ler . . . Italien i svensk dikt. 1956. (*Where the Rose is Smiling . . . Italy in Swedish Poetry.* An anthology.)
Dikter 1949–1955. 1958. (*Poems 1949–1955.*)
Berömda franska berättare i urval av Gunnar Ekelöf och Östen Sjöstrand. Folket i Bilds förlag, Stockholm, 1957. (*Famous French Fiction,* selected by Gunnar Ekelöf and Östen Sjöstrand.)
Hemlöshet och hem. Dikter. 1958. (*Homelessness and Home. Poems.*)
Världen skapas varje dag. Essäer. 1960. (*The World is Created Every Day. Essays.*)
En rucklares väg. Opera i tre akter av Stravinskij. Svensk text av Östen Sjöstrand. 1961. (Translation of W. H. Auden's and Ch. Kallman's *The Rake's Progress.*)
De gåtfulla hindren och andra dikter. 1961. (*The Enigmatic Obstacles and Other Poems.*)
Gästabudet. Drama till musik av Sven-Erik Bäck. 1962. (*The Banquet. Opera book.*)
En vinter i Norden. Dikter. 1963. (*A Winter in the North. Poems.*)

167

I vattumannens tecken. Dikter. 1967. (*In the Sign of Aquarius. Poems.*)

Georg Friedrich Händels Messias. Sveriges Radios förlag, Stockholm, 1968. (The original English text and a Swedish translation and a preface by Östen Sjöstrand.)

Fransk lyrik. 1969. (*French Poetry.* An anthology of Swedish translations, several of them by Sjöstrand himself.)

Ensamma stjärnor, en gemensam horisont. Dikter i urval. 1970. (*Solitary Stars, a Common Horizon. Selected Poems.*)

Yves Bonnefoy: Dikter, i svensk tolkning av Östen Sjöstrand. 1971. (*Yves Bonnefoy: Poems* in Swedish translation by Östen Sjöstrand.)

Fantasins nödvändighet. Författarförlaget, Gothenburg, 1971. (*The Necessity of Imagination.* Essays.)

Jannis Ritsos: Åtbörder, urval och tolkning av Theodor Kallifatides och Östen Sjöstrand. Wahlström & Widstrand, Stockholm, 1971. (*Jannis Ritsos: Gestures,* selected and translated by Theodor Kallifatides and Östen Sjöstrand.)

Drömmen är ingen fasad. Dikter. 1971. (*The Dream is No Façade. Poems.*)

Ola Hansson: Dikter, urval och inledning av Östen Sjöstrand. FIB:s Lyrikklubb, Stockholm, 1972. (*Ola Hansson: Poems,* selected and prefaced by Östen Sjöstrand.)

B. *Poems in English translation by Robin Fulton*

In Magazines:

Spirit XXXIX (2) (Summer 1972) Seton Hall University, South Orange, N.J. 07079

Moln efter moln	Cloud upon cloud
Detta alltför utsatta hjärta	This all too exposed heart
En förhomerisk mur	A prehomeric wall
Sidoblick	Sideglance
Favola	Fable
Brinnande alfabet	Burning alphabet
Den enda stunden	The very moment
En hållfasthetslära	The study of stress
Återbesök	Return visit
Den nya kunskapen	The new knowledge
Den nya fattigdomen	The new poverty
De nödvändiga motstroferna	The necessary antistrophes
Inte ett epitafium	Not an epitaph
Inte en epilog	Not an epilogue

Denver Quarterly VII (3) (Autumn 1972) University of Denver, Colorado 80210

Varje partikel har hela universum till verksamhetsområde	Each particle has the whole universe for its field of activity
I begynnelsen, ännu	In the beginning, still
Tankar inför en påvlig galär	Thoughts before a papal galley

Mundus Artium VI (I) (Winter 1972–73) Ohio University, Athens, Ohio 45701

Motsatser, motljus	Counter-statements, contrary lights
Samtal	Conversation
Motbilder	Counter-images

Lines Review 44 (Spring 1973) Macdonald, Loanhead, Midlothian, Scotland

Agamemnons rop	Agamemnon's cry
Tiden gick in i vattumannens tecken	Time entered the sign of Aquarius

Decal 3 (Winter 1972–73) 52 Dan-y-Coed Road, Cardiff, Wales.

Från Nordafrika	From North Africa
Till de yttersta	For those at the Limit
Utflöden	Outflows
Den gömda musiken	The Hidden Music
Till diktens föderska	To the Bearer of Poetry

C. *Books*

The Hidden Music. Selected, translated and introduced by Robin Fulton. Bilingual text. With a "credo" drawn from Sjöstrand's writings. Published by Oleander Press, 210 Fifth Avenue, New York 10010.

ur *Främmande mörker, främmande ljus* (1955)	*Strange Darkness, Strange Light*
Slättlandskap	Landscape of the Plain
Från Nordafrika	From North Africa
Till de yttersta	For those at the Limit
ur *De gåtfulla hindren* (1961)	*The Enigmatic Obstacles*
Moln efter moln	Cloud upon Cloud
ur *En vinter i Norden* (1963)	*A Winter in the North*

Genom de sammanslående   Through the Clashing Rocks
  klipporna
Utflöden   Outflows
ur *I vattumannens tecken* (1967)   *In the Sign of Aquarius*
Visheten   Wisdom
Varje partikel har hela universum   Each particle has the Whole Uni-
  till verksamhetsområde   verse for its Field of Activity
Irrfärder   Odysseys
Brinnande alfabet   Burning Alphabet
Pesten och den stora lyckan   The Plague and Good Fortune
I begynnelsen, ännu   In the Beginning, still
En förklaringsdag   A Day of Clarification
Agamemnons rop   Agamemnon's Cry
Tiden gick in i vattumannens   Time Entered the Sign of
  tecken   Aquarius
Den nya kunskapen   The New Knowledge
Den gömda musiken   The Hidden Music
Hänförelsens lagar   The Laws of Exultation
Tankar inför en påvlig galär   Thoughts before a Papal Galley
De nödvändiga motstroferna   The Necessary Antistrophes
Inte ett epitafium   Not an Epitaph
Inte en epilog   Not an Epilogue
Till diktens föderska   To the Bearer of Poetry
ur *Drömmen är ingen fasad*   *The Dream is no Façade*
  (1971)
Motsatser, motljus   Counter-Statements, Contrary
                                         Lights
Samtal   Conversation
Motbilder   Counter-images

Index

171